Alexander the Great Uncovered: A Journey Beyond the Battlefield

Myrddin Sage

Published by Myrddin Sage, 2024.

While every precaution has been taken in the preparation of this book, the publisher assumes no responsibility for errors or omissions, or for damages resulting from the use of the information contained herein.

ALEXANDER THE GREAT UNCOVERED: A JOURNEY BEYOND THE BATTLEFIELD

First edition. August 30, 2024.

Copyright © 2024 Myrddin Sage.

ISBN: 979-8227641076

Written by Myrddin Sage.

Also by Myrddin Sage

Echoes of the Ancient: Unlocking the Mysteries of Celtic Myth
Mythic Japan: Unlocking the Legends of Gods and Heroes
Echoes of Enchantment: Navigating the Magic of Celtic Mythology
Warriors and Wizards: The Heroes of Celtic Myth
Echoes of Valhalla: Unveiling the Modern Wisdom of Norse Myths
Gods Among Us: The Power and Intrigue of Roman Mythology
The Sword and the Sage: Unveiling the Truth of Excalibur and Merlin
Myth Unleashed: Rediscovering the Legends of Hercules and the
Pantheon
Echoes of the Gods: Rediscovering the Heroes and Deities of Ancient
Egypt
Ancient Echoes: Embracing Egyptian Wisdom in Our Modern World
Alexander the Great Uncovered: A Journey Beyond the Battlefield

Table of Contents

Dedication

To the curious minds and passionate hearts,

This book is dedicated to the young student who seeks relevance in the dusty pages of history and to the history enthusiast who yearns for a narrative that captures the human drama of the past. Your frustrations and thirst for an engaging, accessible history inspired me to write this book.

I am deeply grateful to my mentors for their wisdom and encouragement, my colleagues for their expertise, and my friends for their unwavering support. Your contributions have enriched this journey.

To you, the reader, thank you for embarking on this voyage. May this book expand your understanding and challenge your perceptions, telling a story with a heartbeat. This is for those who crave history as a subject and as a living, breathing narrative.

With gratitude, Myrddin Sage

Alexander the Great Uncovered: A Journey Beyond the Battlefield

Unlock the Secrets of a Legendary Empire and Its Leader in Days, Without the Historical Drudge

Preface

"I am not afraid of an army of lions led by a sheep; I am afraid of an army of sheep led by a lion." — Alexander the Great.

Few figures are as enigmatic and influential in the tapestry of history as Alexander the Great. His conquests reshaped the world, but the essence of the man behind the legend often remains obscured by the sands of time. This book invites readers to journey beyond the battlefield into the heart and mind of one of history's most legendary leaders.

At the core of this narrative lies a simple yet profound aim: to present Alexander not just as a historical figure but as a source of inspiration, a window into an era of monumental change, and a reflection on human potential. I embarked on this project driven by the curiosity that many of you share—a longing to connect with the past in a way that feels alive and immediate rather than a collection of dates and impersonal events.

Imagine, for a moment, a young student struggling to find relevance in the dusty pages of an ancient history textbook or a history enthusiast who always felt that traditional narratives didn't quite capture the human drama of times gone by. These are the individuals who inspired me to write this book. Their frustrations echoed my own experiences and highlighted a common thirst for a history that is not only accessible but deeply engaging.

In crafting this book, I drew upon classical texts and modern historians' insights, blending these with vivid storytelling to breathe life into Alexander's world. My journey was enriched by mentors who provided wisdom and encouragement, colleagues who shared their expertise, and friends who offered unwavering support.

Thank you to each of you who has picked up this volume. You've chosen to embark on a voyage that promises to expand your understanding and challenge your perceptions. This book is for those passionate about history yet craving a story told with a heartbeat. It assumes no prior expertise, only curiosity and a desire to explore.

As we flip through these pages together, we'll uncover the strategies that made Alexander a great leader and delve into the cultural exchanges sparked by his conquests. We will witness his battles, yes, but also walk the bustling streets of Babylon and stand under the vast expanse of Persian skies, feeling the pulse of ancient civilizations.

Thank you for bringing your enthusiasm and spirit of discovery to this reading. I invite you to continue engaging with Alexander's story as it unfolds and find the same inspiration that has captivated generations. Let's rediscover history—not just as it happened, but as it felt.

Chapter 1: The Empire Whisperer: Beyond the Battlefields

When Cultures Collide and Blend

Elias strolled through the bustling market of Alexandria, his eyes catching glimpses of vibrant fabrics and his nose teased by the mingling scents of cinnamon and cumin. The city, a melting pot of cultures, buzzed with the energy of a thousand conversations, each in a different tongue yet somehow harmonious. Here, Elias often pondered Alexander's legacy as a conqueror and a unifier of worlds.

In his mind, Elias retraced Alexander the Great's steps, imagining him not with sword drawn but with hand extended. He saw him at wedding feasts, binding himself to foreign princesses as political ploys and sincere gestures toward integration. Each union was like planting a seed in fertile soil—a seed that would sprout into new ideas and customs that would travel across continents.

As he passed a stall selling Greek pottery alongside Egyptian papyrus scrolls, Elias reflected on how these objects were metaphors for their times—distinct yet displayed together in harmony. He thought about how this approach to governance had sown the seeds for the Hellenistic period, an era marked by unprecedented cultural and intellectual exchanges.

A child ran past him, nearly toppling a stack of scrolls. A smile softened the stall owner's sharp rebuke as he righted his wares. This interruption jolted Elias back from ancient times to the present moment. The sun dipped lower in the sky, casting long shadows between the columns that lined the marketplace.

Elias wondered how much today's leaders could learn from Alexander's example. Could modern societies embrace such integration without losing their identity? Or was it inevitable for some essence to be lost in exchange for something new? As he watched people of all descents barter and exchange ideas at stalls, he realized they were living parts of an ongoing story that started long ago.

What does it indeed mean to integrate cultures without erasing them?

Unveiling the Master of Multiculturalism

When reflecting on Alexander the Great, images of epic battles and unyielding conquests often dominate the narrative. Yet, to truly grasp his legacy, one must look beyond the battlefields to his profound role as a cultural integrator. His strategic marriages, adoption of local customs, and genuine interest in fostering an environment of multiculturalism paint a picture of a leader whose influence extended far beyond military achievements. This chapter delves into how Alexander didn't just build an empire through force but nurtured it through wisdom and respect for diversity.

The Architect of Integration

At the heart of Alexander's success was his visionary approach to governance. Unlike many conquerors who sought to impose their culture upon their conquests, Alexander was keenly aware that the sustainability of his vast empire depended on a more inclusive approach. He respected and embraced the customs and traditions of the lands he conquered. This strategic yet genuine respect helped pacify subdued cities and foster loyalty among diverse groups.

Marriages as Bridges

Alexander's marriages were not merely political alliances but profound statements of integration and respect for local traditions. By marrying Roxana, a Bactrian princess, he did not just ally with a new region; he showed his willingness to intertwine his life and legacy with those he ruled over. These unions' symbolic gestures spoke volumes about his intentions toward creating a harmonious multicultural empire.

Seeds of the Hellenistic Period

The lasting impact of Alexander's policies can be seen in the flourishing of the Hellenistic period—a time characterized by an incredible exchange of ideas, art, and culture across a vast area from Greece to India. By laying down the multicultural foundations, Alexander set the stage for a period that would see significant advancements in science, philosophy, and arts—his foresight in integrating various cultures under one administrative framework allowed for an unprecedented flow of knowledge.

Why This Matters

Understanding Alexander's role as a proactive cultural integrator provides invaluable insights into how leaders can successfully manage diverse societies. It's not merely about conquest but about creating a sustainable system where multiple cultures can coexist and enrich each other. This chapter aims to shift focus from Alexander's military exploits to his strategic cultural integrations, arguably leaving a more enduring legacy than his battles.

In exploring these themes, we see Alexander not just as a historical figure but as a timeless example of effective leadership in diversity management. His story offers lessons on the power of respectful cultural integration that are relevant even today's globalized world.

By embarking on this journey beyond the battlefield with Alexander, readers will uncover layers of his persona often overshadowed by his military prowess. This exploration is not just about understanding history; it's about drawing lessons from it that apply to modern leadership challenges, making it an enlightening read for anyone interested in history, leadership, or cultural studies.

As we proceed through this narrative, let us keep an open mind to learn from Alexander's governance and cultural integration strategies—strategies that transformed him from merely being a conqueror to becoming *The Empire Whisperer*. This reflective journey promises historical insights and inspiring lessons in leadership and unity.

Alexander the Great's legacy extends far beyond the battlefields he conquered. While his military conquests are well-documented, his role as a proactive cultural integrator is equally remarkable.

Alexander's approach to governance went beyond mere domination; he sought to understand and incorporate the customs and traditions of the diverse regions he conquered. This mindset of cultural integration set him apart from many conquerors of his time, laying the foundation for a more inclusive and interconnected empire.

Alexander's ability to embrace local customs and marry foreign princesses was crucial in fostering multiculturalism within his empire. Alexander formed political alliances by marrying women from different regions and was willing to bridge cultural divides. These marriages symbolized unity and acceptance, sending a powerful message of inclusivity throughout his vast territories.

The impact of Alexander's cultural integration extended far beyond his lifetime. His efforts laid the groundwork for the Hellenistic period, a time known for its rich cultural exchanges and intellectual advancements. By encouraging interaction between Greek, Persian, Egyptian, and other cultures, Alexander created an environment where ideas could flourish and knowledge could spread freely.

One of Alexander's most significant strengths lay in his ability to learn from the diverse cultures he encountered. Rather than imposing Greek customs on conquered peoples, he adapted and incorporated aspects of their traditions into his own rule. This approach promoted harmony within his empire and allowed a more nuanced understanding of the world.

By embracing multiculturalism, Alexander paved the way for future generations to appreciate the value of diversity. His legacy serves as a reminder that true strength lies in unity, cooperation, and mutual respect among different cultures. In a world often divided by differences, Alexander's example offers a timeless lesson in the power of cultural integration and collaboration.

Please continue reading to learn how Alexander's marriages and adoption of local customs shaped the regions he conquered.

Throughout history, Alexander the Great's impact on the regions he conquered went far beyond military conquests. His strategic marriages and adoption of local customs played a significant role in shaping the cultures of these lands. Alexander solidified his rule by marrying into local royal families and creating ties that bound different cultures together. ***His marriages were not just political alliances but bridges between diverse societies***, fostering a sense of unity and cooperation.

Alexander's willingness to adopt and integrate local customs into his empire showcased his adaptability and respect for different cultures. Instead of imposing Greek traditions on conquered territories, he embraced the practices of the people he ruled. This approach helped ease tensions and promote cultural exchange, laying the foundation for a more harmonious coexistence among various ethnic groups.

The impact of Alexander's marriages extended beyond mere diplomatic gestures. By marrying women from different regions, he symbolized unity and acceptance, sending his subjects a powerful message of inclusivity. These unions were about political strategy and creating a sense of shared identity among diverse populations under his rule.

His marriages catalyzed cultural diffusion, leading to the blending of traditions and ideas across different regions. The offspring of these unions grew up with a unique blend of influences, contributing to the richness and diversity of the Hellenistic world that emerged after Alexander's reign.

By embracing multiculturalism through his marriages and adopting local customs, Alexander laid the groundwork for a more interconnected world where ideas could flow freely across borders. This openness to diversity was a critical factor in the cultural flourishing that characterized the Hellenistic period, marked by artistic, scientific, and philosophical advancements that transcended traditional boundaries.

Alexander's approach to governance through marriage alliances and cultural integration was revolutionary. Instead of imposing a homogenized culture on his vast empire, he celebrated diversity and encouraged cross-cultural interactions. This forward-thinking mindset set the stage for an era of intellectual exchange and innovation that shaped the future of Western civilization.

In essence, *Alexander's marriages and adoption of local customs were not just political maneuvers but visionary steps toward building a more inclusive and interconnected world.* His legacy as a proactive cultural integrator resonates today, reminding us of the power of embracing diversity and fostering understanding among different cultures.

The multicultural foundations laid during Alexander's reign had a profound and lasting impact on the Hellenistic period that followed. *Alexander's approach to governance, which embraced local customs and encouraged cultural exchanges, set the stage for a new era of intellectual and artistic flourishing.* By blending the best of various cultures under his rule, he created a fertile ground where innovation and creativity could thrive. This fusion of ideas and traditions resulted in a rich tapestry of knowledge that would shape the world for centuries.

The Hellenistic period, characterized by its diverse influences and cosmopolitan nature, was a direct outcome of Alexander's vision for a unified empire. The interactions between different cultures during his reign paved the way for unprecedented cultural exchange. Greek philosophy, art, and science mingled with Eastern traditions, creating a vibrant melting pot of ideas that fueled advancements in various fields. *This cultural synthesis laid the foundation for developing new philosophies, artistic styles, and scientific discoveries that would shape history.*

Alexander's legacy of multiculturalism endured long after his death, influencing not only the territories he conquered but future generations worldwide. Blending Greek, Persian, Egyptian, and other cultures created a legacy of tolerance and understanding transcending borders. *This legacy inspired future empires and civilizations to embrace diversity and seek common ground with others*, leading to further exchanges of knowledge and ideas across continents.

The Hellenistic period's emphasis on intellectual pursuits and cultural integration can be traced back to Alexander's reign, where he laid the groundwork for such endeavors through his policies and personal actions. His marriages to foreign princesses symbolized a commitment to uniting different cultures through familial ties, promoting peace and cooperation among diverse peoples. *This approach solidified his rule and paved the way for a more inclusive society where individuals from various backgrounds could thrive.*

In essence, Alexander's proactive embrace of multiculturalism was not just a political strategy but a visionary approach to fostering harmony and progress among different civilizations. His legacy as an empire whisperer who bridged cultural divides continues to resonate in modern times as societies strive to find common ground amidst diversity. *The lessons learned from his reign echo through history as a reminder of the power of unity in driving innovation, creativity, and mutual understanding across nations and ages.*

His military conquests often overshadow Alexander the Great's legacy. Still, a deeper exploration reveals his extraordinary role as a cultural integrator. His proactive approach in adopting local customs and forming matrimonial alliances was not merely a strategy for political stability but a visionary move towards multicultural integration. This facet of his leadership sowed the seeds for a new era where diverse cultures could converge and flourish together, laying a robust foundation for the Hellenistic period.

Alexander's genius lies in his dual role as a conqueror and a unifier. Far from mere political maneuvers, his marriages were profound gestures of respect and acceptance toward the cultures he encountered. By embracing these customs, Alexander did not just rule; he learned and adapted, fostering an environment where Greek and local cultures could enrich each other.

Reflecting on these actions today, we see a leader whose strategies were as much about hearts and minds as they were about lands and riches. His multicultural foundations impacted the immediate socio-political landscape and propelled the Hellenistic period into a flourishing epoch known for its cultural, intellectual, and artistic exchanges.

As we progress through this book, we will continue to uncover layers of Alexander's strategies and their long-lasting effects on the world. Each chapter promises to reveal more about how his dynamic approach to leadership and governance has lessons that remain relevant in today's globalized society.

Understanding Alexander's deep commitment to cultural integration allows readers to reflect on the importance of cultural respect and integration in their lives. This exploration is not just about historical facts but about understanding the profound impacts of leadership and cultural openness.

Embark on this journey with us, where history meets wisdom, and discover how the past can illuminate paths toward a better understanding of leadership and coexistence. Let's continue to unravel the secrets behind Alexander the Great, finding inspiration in his story that may guide us in our present and future endeavors.

Chapter 2: The Art of War and Wisdom: Strategic Leadership Unveiled

Can Timeless Tactics Forge Future Leaders?

In the dimly lit room of a modern university, a professor named Thomas leaned over his cluttered desk, his eyes tracing the lines of an ancient text about Alexander the Great. The soft hum of the air conditioning blended with the distant laughter of students outside, creating a backdrop to his deep concentration. Thomas was preparing for his following lecture on strategic leadership, drawing parallels between historical military tactics and contemporary business strategies.

As he pondered over Alexander's maneuvers at Gaugamela, where strategy and flexibility had turned the tides against seemingly insurmountable odds, Thomas reflected on how these principles could be applied to modern corporate battles. The clock ticked audibly, marking the passage of time yet standing as a testament to the timeless nature of these lessons.

Outside, leaves rustled as a gentle breeze swept through the campus, whispering of change and challenges. Thomas felt a connection across millennia; like Alexander, today's leaders faced their own Persia to conquer—markets full of competitors and ever-evolving technologies. His mind wandered to a recent board meeting where innovative ideas clashed with traditional approaches, echoing the Macedonian phalanx breaking through conventional lines.

A student knocked timidly on the open door, her interruption pulling Thomas back from ancient battlefields to present concerns.

She asked about applying historical examples to modern-day leadership challenges for her thesis. As they discussed Alexander's ability to inspire and lead from the front, Thomas saw a spark in her eyes — the kind that comes from connecting deeply with an idea that resonates.

He shared how true leaders today still need that blend of courage and cunning, wisdom in choosing battles, and the ability to pivot strategies swiftly in response to unforeseen circumstances. The discussion wandered from military tactics to boardroom strategies, each example shining light on universal truths about human nature and leadership.

As she left, filled with ideas and enthusiasm for her project, Thomas glanced back at his scattered books — some open with maps showing troop movements that changed history. He smiled faintly at the thought: if lessons from dusty pages could ignite future leadership fires, what would be their first test in this rapidly changing world?

How might leaders today harness ancient wisdom like Alexander's to navigate and shape tomorrow's uncertainties?

Lessons from the Past, Leadership for the Future

History is often said to be our most outstanding teacher, and nowhere is this truer than the study of Alexander the Great's strategic genius. Today's leaders, whether steering multinational corporations or small teams, can draw valuable lessons from Alexander's ancient battlefields. His campaigns across diverse terrains and against varied foes illuminate timeless leadership, adaptability, and vision strategies that remain pertinent in navigating our modern complexities.

The Timeless Strategic Playbook

Alexander's conquests were not merely by brute force; they were masterclasses in strategic planning and tactical flexibility. His ability to foresee changes in scenarios and adapt swiftly was extraordinary. This chapter delves into how such foresight and flexibility can be translated into today's leadership challenges—where the ability to pivot and innovate is more crucial than ever.

Leading from the Front

A hallmark of Alexander's leadership was his presence on the front lines, standing shoulder-to-shoulder with his men. This visible leadership inspired loyalty and allowed him to make quick, informed decisions. In our current age, where leaders are often removed from core operations, Alexander's example underscores the value of being deeply involved and responsive to an organization's immediate needs.

Battles as Case Studies

Specific battles under Alexander's command, such as Gaugamela and Hydaspes, showcase his strategic depth and versatility. These confrontations reveal how he assessed risks, managed resources, and exploited enemy weaknesses—skills pertinent to today's high-stakes decision-making scenario. By examining these battles, we can extract principles of resource allocation, risk management, and competitive strategy applicable to business ventures and personal challenges.

Modern Applications

What does it mean to lead a team against seemingly insurmountable odds? How can one harness the collective strength of a diverse group to achieve a common goal? These questions are at the heart of this exploration as we apply Alexander's strategies to contemporary settings. From boardrooms to battlegrounds, understanding the dynamics of effective leadership can ignite transformative changes.

Through this insightful journey into Alexander's tactical mind, readers will uncover historical facts and living strategies that can be tailored to their leadership styles and challenges.

Whether it's running a company or spearheading a community project, the principles distilled from Alexander's campaigns offer a blueprint for robust strategic planning and inspirational leadership.

Reflecting on these age-old tactics will inspire current and future leaders to think broadly and act wisely as they navigate their professional landscapes. Embracing these lessons means stepping beyond traditional boundaries—much like Alexander himself—and moving towards achieving greatness in their realms.

Thus, it unfolds a narrative that bridges millennia, an exploration that transcends mere historical analysis to become a practical guide for enduring leadership excellence. Let us embark on this reflective journey together, learning from one of history's most outstanding leaders to enhance our capabilities in leading effectively amidst today's global challenges.

Alexander the Great's military strategies continue to resonate with contemporary leadership challenges, offering timeless lessons in strategic thinking and decision-making. Despite the vast temporal gulf, Alexander's maneuvers on the battlefield remain a wellspring of insight for modern leaders navigating complex environments.

His ability to adapt swiftly to changing circumstances, coupled with his audacious leadership style, enabled him to triumph over seemingly insurmountable odds, showcasing the enduring relevance of his tactics.

From Alexander's playbook, today's leaders can glean valuable lessons in agility and resilience. In an ever-evolving landscape where unpredictability is the norm, pivoting swiftly in response to new information or obstacles is paramount. Alexander's capacity to adjust his strategies on the fly is a poignant reminder of the importance of flexibility in leadership. By remaining open to change and ready to recalibrate plans, leaders can enhance their chances of success in dynamic environments when necessary.

Moreover, Alexander's penchant for leading from the front underscores the significance of hands-on involvement and personal accountability in leadership roles. By setting an example through direct engagement and sharing the risks faced by their team, leaders can inspire trust and foster a sense of camaraderie within their ranks. This approach bolsters morale and instills confidence in followers, creating a cohesive unit capable of tackling challenges collectively.

The art of war, as exemplified by Alexander, emphasizes the value of strategic foresight and calculated risk-taking. Alexander achieved remarkable feats that defied conventional wisdom by meticulously planning his campaigns while remaining attuned to opportunities for bold moves. This blend of meticulous preparation and daring execution is a blueprint for contemporary leaders seeking to navigate competitive landscapes with finesse.

Continue reading how specific battles showcase Alexander's tactical flexibility and leadership prowess.

Alexander's military campaigns were marked by battles showcasing his remarkable tactical flexibility and exceptional leadership skills. One such battle was the Battle of Issus, where Alexander faced off against the Persian king Darius III. Despite being outnumbered, Alexander's strategic brilliance and quick decision-making allowed him to secure a decisive victory. This battle is a testament to *Alexander's ability to adapt to changing circumstances and boldly move in the face of adversity.*

Another significant engagement was the Battle of Gaugamela, often regarded as one of Alexander's most impressive victories.

Faced with an enormous Persian army led by Darius III, Alexander once again demonstrated his strategic acumen by devising a plan that exploited his opponent's weaknesses. *His willingness to take calculated risks and his capacity to inspire his troops in the heat of battle were crucial factors in securing triumph.*

The Siege of Tyre stands out as a testament to Alexander's determination and innovative tactics. With an island city fortified against traditional siege methods, Alexander engineered a groundbreaking solution by constructing a causeway to reach the city walls. This unconventional approach highlights *Alexander's problem-solving creativity and ability to think outside the box when facing challenges.*

At the Battle of Hydaspes, Alexander faced King Porus and his formidable army in a grueling conflict that tested his leadership skills to their limits. Despite facing harsh terrain and fierce resistance from Porus' forces, Alexander's strategic maneuvering and unwavering resolve enabled him to emerge victorious. This battle underscores *Alexander's resilience in the face of adversity and his capacity to inspire loyalty and bravery in his troops.*

The Battle of Granicus is another example of Alexander's tactical brilliance and fearless leadership. When confronted with a river crossing that posed a significant challenge, Alexander led from the front, inspiring his soldiers to follow him into battle. His hands-on approach and willingness to share risks with his men exemplify *the kind of leader who leads by example and earns the respect and admiration of those under his command.*

In each of these battles, Alexander's ability to adapt to changing circumstances, think creatively, inspire his troops, and lead from the front was pivotal to securing victory. His legacy as a strategic genius and charismatic leader continues to resonate today, offering valuable lessons for contemporary leaders facing complex challenges. By studying Alexander's military campaigns, modern leaders can glean insights into effective decision-making, strategic planning, and inspiring teamwork in pursuit of shared goals.

Descriptive Framework

Understanding Alexander, the Great's leadership style and military tactics reveals a comprehensive framework that can be applied to modern strategic planning. This framework delves into Alexander's pivotal battles, leadership qualities, and adaptability and explains how these lessons can be extrapolated to contemporary contexts.

By dissecting each component of this framework, we gain insights into effective leadership strategies that stand the test of time.

Key Battles Analysis

Alexander's key battles were not merely displays of brute force but intricate maneuvers that utilized terrain, troop formations, and psychological strategies. By studying these battles, such as the Battle of Gaugamela, we uncover the importance of strategic positioning and leveraging the environment to gain an advantage.

This component highlights the significance of meticulous planning and tactical execution in achieving victory.

Leadership Qualities

Alexander's ability to inspire loyalty and courage among his troops was a hallmark of his leadership. His charisma and lead-from-the-front approach instilled a sense of purpose and camaraderie within his army. This aspect underscores the vital role of emotional intelligence and leading by example in fostering a cohesive and motivated team.

Adaptability

One of Alexander's most remarkable traits was his adaptability in changing tactics based on the situation. This flexibility mirrors agile project management principles, emphasizing the need to pivot swiftly in response to evolving circumstances. By being open to adjusting strategies on the fly, leaders can navigate complex challenges with agility and precision.

Application in Modern Contexts

By assessing contemporary leadership challenges through Alexander's strategies, individuals can gain a structured approach to problem-solving. Drawing parallels between historical events and present-day scenarios allows for a deeper understanding of effective decision-making processes. Applying these insights in business or political leadership will enable leaders to navigate uncertainty clearly and purposefully.

This framework encapsulates Alexander the Great's strategic leadership style, offering timeless lessons that resonate across centuries. By integrating elements of critical battle analysis, leadership qualities, adaptability, and modern applications, individuals can glean valuable insights into effective leadership practices that transcend historical boundaries.

Step Up Your Game: The Alexander Technique for Modern Leaders

Understanding Alexander the Great's time-tested strategies illuminates the brilliance of his tactical maneuvers and provides a robust framework for addressing today's leadership challenges. By dissecting his approaches, we uncover principles that transcend the battlegrounds of ancient empires and resonate deeply with contemporary strategic leadership.

Step 1: Understanding the Relevance of Alexander's Military Strategies

Firstly, grasp the significance of Alexander's strategies in today's complex leadership landscape. His adaptability and foresight in military engagements mirror the dynamic decision-making required in modern business or organizational contexts. Reflect on these strategies to discern how they can be integrated into current practices, fostering a culture of resilience and proactive leadership.

Step 2: Analyzing Specific Battles Showcasing Tactical Flexibility

Next, delve into specific instances of Alexander's campaigns to identify critical elements of his tactical flexibility. Note how his ability to shift tactics mid-battle, based on real-time observations, sets a precedent for modern leaders to remain agile and responsive.

This analysis highlights historical military genius and encourages a flexible approach to today's unpredictable market and operational challenges.

Step 3: Creating Modern Strategic Plans Based on Alexander's Leadership Style

Applying Alexander's frontline leadership style to contemporary strategic planning builds on your insights. Consider how his principles of clear communication, decisive action, and unwavering confidence can enhance your leadership approach. By embodying these qualities, you can inspire and direct teams with a clarity and conviction that mirrors Alexander's.

Step 4: Applying Alexander's Leadership Style in Contemporary Scenarios

Finally, brainstorm practical applications of Alexander's leadership in modern scenarios. Whether leading a small team or an entire organization, consider how his ethos of leading by example and fostering loyalty can translate into your daily leadership practices.

Discuss these ideas with peers to expand their potential and adapt them to fit various industries and organizational cultures.

By systematically exploring these steps, you pay homage to one of history's most outstanding leaders and equip yourself with a potent strategic toolkit that is both venerable and vastly applicable.

Embrace these lessons to navigate the complexities of modern leadership with the same courage and intelligence that Alexander demonstrated through his conquests.

Chapter 3: From Conquests to Chronicles: Storytelling as a Historical Lens

Can the Art of Storytelling Change Our Perception of History?

In the quiet confines of a small study lined with shelves burdened by history books, Thomas, a middle-aged history teacher, sat contemplating the power of narrative. A beam of sunlight pierced through the window, casting long shadows across the wooden floor and highlighting dust motes dancing like tiny specters in the air.

The clock ticked steadily, marking time in a room otherwise wrapped in silence.

Thomas leaned back in his chair, his fingers tentatively touching the spine of a book titled *"Alexander the Great: A Life in Legend."*

His mind wandered to tomorrow's lesson; he was determined to break away from the monotony of dates and battles that often glazed over his students' eyes. The story of Alexander — not just his conquests but his character, dreams, and doubts — could perhaps ignite a spark of interest. He imagined weaving tales that painted Alexander not merely as a figure in textbooks but as a living entity who once had ambitions and fears much like them.

Outside, children's laughter floated up from the street below, pulling Thomas back from ancient Macedon to his quiet town. He smiled faintly, realizing how stories had shaped his understanding of people and events throughout his life. Why should teaching history be any different? Could he help his students see themselves reflected in the past and learn lessons about resilience and ambition through Alexander's extraordinary yet human story?

As he flipped through pages filled with accounts of battles and diplomacy, Thomas envisioned tomorrow's class differently. He would ask them what they thought Alexander felt when he stood before Thebes or crossed the Hellespont. What fears did he harbor?

What dreams drove him onward far from home?

Could seeing history through this lens help students connect more deeply with those who shaped our world? Would they remember these stories better than any date or name could ever hope to be remembered?

Unraveling the Tapestry of History Through Stories

When we speak of Alexander the Great, images of battles and conquests might emerge—spectacular narratives set in distant lands under ancient skies. Yet, an equally compelling story is woven in the quieter threads of these tales. In this exploration, we pivot from the clashing of swords to the crafting of sentences, understanding that *storytelling* profoundly shapes our perception of historical figures. This approach doesn't just add layers to what we know; it transforms Alexander from a figure of antiquity into a mirror reflecting timeless human struggles and aspirations.

The Power of Narrative in History

Historical accounts are often perceived as dry compilations of facts and dates, yet they come alive through storytelling. By examining how narratives have sculpted our understanding of Alexander, we uncover not just a man leading armies but also a symbol of human ambition and complexity. This chapter delves into the narrative techniques that transform the mosaic of Alexander's campaigns into a relatable and engaging saga that resonates with modern sensibilities.

Crafting Compelling Characters from Historical Figures

Alexander's image as a ruthless conqueror or a visionary leader largely depends on who tells his story and how. Here, we identify vital narrative strategies that make his history not only accessible but also gripping. Through anecdotes and reconstructed dialogues, historians and storytellers create a persona that viewers can love or loathe, pity or admire—often forgetting these emotions arise from historical acts and their portrayal.

Character and Resolve: The Human Core in Historical Narratives

At the heart of any memorable story are characters that exhibit relatable human qualities—courage, fear, ambition. Reflecting on this aspect reveals why stories about Alexander continue to captivate him: they showcase his strategic brilliance and his personal vulnerabilities and triumphs. These elements highlight the importance of human character and resolve, turning historical accounts into lessons on human nature.

By engaging with these facets, we step beyond the conventional boundaries of historical scholarship. We see Alexander's life as a narrative rich with universal and enduring themes of power, legacy, and human frailty. This approach does more than make learning about him enjoyable; it makes it unforgettable because it connects deeply with our collective psyche.

Through this lens, history is no longer just about the past; it's about understanding the complexities of human behavior and motivations—insights as relevant today as they were in Alexander's time. The stories we tell about historical figures do more than recount what they did; they influence how we think about them and, by extension, how we understand ourselves.

In embracing this narrative-driven exploration of history, we enrich our knowledge and gain deeper insights into what drives us as humans. Thus, storytelling in history is not merely educational; it's transformative—a powerful tool that brings ancient worlds to vivid life and makes their lessons applicable to our own.

Storytelling has the incredible power to transform our understanding of historical figures like Alexander the Great. By weaving together facts and events into a cohesive narrative, history becomes more than just a series of dates and conquests. It becomes a living, breathing story that captures our attention and sparks our imagination. Through storytelling, we can delve deeper into the psyche of Alexander, exploring not just what he did but why he did it. This narrative approach humanizes historical figures, allowing us to relate to their struggles, triumphs, and complexities on a personal level.

Immersing ourselves in Alexander's story enables us to see beyond the surface of his conquests. We begin to appreciate his challenges, decisions, and impact on the world around him. Instead of viewing him as a distant figure from the past, storytelling brings Alexander to life as a multifaceted individual with hopes, fears, and aspirations. This shift in perspective allows us to connect with him on a deeper level, fostering empathy and understanding of the complexities of his character.

Through storytelling, we can uncover the nuances of Alexander's personality and motivations. We see him as a conqueror, a visionary leader driven by ambition and a desire for greatness. By delving into his struggles and relationships, we gain insight into the man behind the legend. This intimate portrayal humanizes Alexander, making him more relatable and understandable to modern audiences.

One of the most compelling aspects of storytelling is its ability to evoke emotion and empathy in readers. As we follow Alexander's journey through triumphs and setbacks, we become emotionally invested in his story. We share in his joys and sorrows, his victories and defeats. This emotional connection deepens our appreciation for the challenges he faced and the legacy he left behind. Through storytelling, history comes alive in a way that engages our hearts and minds.

By presenting history through storytelling, we invite readers to step into the shoes of historical figures like Alexander. We encourage them to see the world through his eyes, to experience his triumphs and struggles firsthand. This immersive approach educates and entertains, making learning about history an engaging and enriching experience. Through storytelling, we bridge the gap between past and present, connecting with figures from antiquity in a way that feels immediate and relevant.

Dive deeper into the narrative techniques that bring Alexander's story to life...

Narrative techniques are crucial in shaping historical accounts, making figures like Alexander the Great come alive through storytelling. By weaving together crucial elements such as characterization, plot development, and thematic exploration, historians can present a more compelling and relatable version of the past.

Characterization is particularly vital in bringing historical figures to life. When describing Alexander, highlighting his ambition, courage, and leadership qualities helps readers connect with his persona on a deeper level. *Plot development* is another essential technique that keeps the narrative engaging. Detailing Alexander's conquests, challenges, and triumphs chronologically creates a sense of progression and builds anticipation for the next event.

Thematic exploration adds layers of meaning to historical storytelling. Historians can offer insights into universal truths that resonate across time by delving into themes like power, legacy, and the human condition. These themes serve as *anchors* that ground the narrative and provide readers with points of reflection and introspection. Additionally, incorporating *emotional depth* into the storytelling allows readers to empathize with historical figures like

Alexander on a personal level. Historians make these larger-than-life characters more relatable and human by showcasing their vulnerabilities, fears, and triumphs.

Vivid imagery is another powerful narrative technique that enhances the storytelling experience. Descriptions of battles, landscapes, and court intrigues transport readers to ancient times, immersing them in the world of Alexander and his empire.

Through sensory language that appeals to sight, sound, smell, taste, and touch, historians create a rich tapestry of historical events that feel vivid and immediate. This approach educates and entertains, making the learning process enjoyable and memorable for readers.

Moreover, *foreshadowing* is an effective technique that adds suspense and intrigue to historical narratives. By hinting at future events or outcomes early in the story, historians create anticipation and keep readers invested in the unfolding tale of Alexander's life.

Foreshadowing allows for subtle connections between past actions and their consequences, encouraging readers to think critically about historical cause-and-effect relationships.

In essence, by employing diverse narrative techniques such as characterization, plot development, thematic exploration, vivid imagery, emotional depth, and foreshadowing, historians can transform historical accounts into captivating stories that resonate with readers on a profound level. These techniques make the history of figures like Alexander more compelling and invite readers to engage with the past in a way that sparks curiosity, empathy, and reflection.

Reflecting on historical narratives reveals the profound impact of human character and resolve in shaping events. As we delve into Alexander the Great's life, we uncover conquests and battles and the intricate tapestry of his personality and determination. *Human characters'* flaws and virtues provide depth to historical figures, making them relatable and compelling to study. Alexander's unwavering resolve to conquer new lands and push boundaries showcases the power of ambition and vision in driving monumental change throughout history.

The importance of human character in historical narratives goes beyond mere storytelling; it mirrors our aspirations, fears, and potential for greatness. When we examine Alexander's leadership qualities, strategic brilliance, and ability to inspire loyalty in his troops, we are not just learning about a distant figure from the past but drawing parallels to our lives. *Resolve*, depicted through Alexander's relentless pursuit of his goals despite insurmountable odds, teaches us about perseverance and dedication in facing adversity.

By exploring human character, we gain insight into the complexities of historical figures like Alexander, moving beyond a superficial understanding to a profound appreciation for their struggles and triumphs. Understanding the motivations behind their actions allows us to empathize with their decisions and challenges, fostering a deeper connection to the past. *Character becomes* a lens through which we can analyze history, uncovering the driving forces behind pivotal moments that have shaped civilizations.

Intertwined with character, resolve forms the backbone of historical narratives, showcasing the resilience and determination required to overcome obstacles and achieve greatness. In Alexander's relentless march across continents, we see not just a military campaign but a testament to human willpower and fortitude. His unwavering determination to leave a lasting legacy echoes through the annals of history, inspiring generations to pursue their dreams with steadfast commitment.

As we reflect on human character and resolve in historical narratives, we are reminded of our capacity for growth and transformation. Just as Alexander's ambition drove him to conquer vast empires, our aspirations can propel us toward personal milestones and societal change. By embracing the lessons embedded in these stories of courage and perseverance, we tap into a wellspring of inspiration that propels us toward our big and small conquests.

In conclusion, when we view history through the lens of human character and resolve, we unlock a treasure trove of wisdom and insight that transcends time. By immersing ourselves in the stories of remarkable individuals like Alexander the Great, we learn about the past and discover valuable lessons that resonate with our present realities. Let us embrace these narratives as beacons guiding us toward a future filled with purpose, courage, and unyielding determination.

As we journey through the historical narratives of figures like Alexander the Great, it becomes clear how *powerful storytelling* shapes our understanding of the past. This chapter has explored the events of Alexander's life and how these events are conveyed, emphasizing that *how* a story is told is as crucial as *what is* said.

As discussed, manipulating narrative techniques bridges the gap between past and present, making Alexander's conquests more than mere historical facts; they become compelling, instructive tales that resonate personally. Through this approach, history is no longer a static, distant recount but a vivid, dynamic narrative that engages and inspires.

Reflecting on the importance of human character and resolve in these stories, we grasp not only Alexander's strategic genius but also his human flaws and virtues. This dual perspective fosters a deeper connection and prompts us to reflect on our own lives and challenges. It's a reminder that behind every historical figure are *real human experiences and* decisions, which continue to influence and teach us today.

By transforming historical accounts into relatable stories, we do more than remember the past—we learn from it. This method not only makes learning about figures like Alexander more enjoyable but also more memorable. It encourages us to think critically about the narratives we accept. It challenges us to look deeper into the stories that shape our understanding of history.

As we move forward in this book, remember the transformative power of storytelling. It's not just about recounting events but about connecting those events to the universal human experience, bringing history to life in a way that is both enlightening and profoundly personal. Let's continue to uncover the layers of Alexander's legacy, keeping in mind that our perceptions are often shaped by how we learn and by *what* we learn.

Chapter 4: An Empire Lost, A Legacy Unbroken

Can Legacy Outlast Empire?

In the dusty expanse of northern Greece, a historian named Elias walked along the ancient ruins of Pella, once the vibrant capital of Macedon and the birthplace of Alexander the Great. The sun hung low, painting long shadows that stretched across crumbling columns and broken pathways, much like the long shadow Alexander himself cast across history.

Elias stopped by a half-toppled stone that might have once been part of a grand archway. He ran his fingers over the cool surface, tracing lines that wind and time had etched. He thought about how Alexander's empire crumbled after his untimely death, much like these stones. Yet, his influence carved deep grooves into the fabric of history that guided the course of cultures and politics long after his cities fell to dust.

As he moved through the ruins, Elias imagined the bustling streets filled with traders from distant lands speaking a Babel of tongues, all brought together under Alexander's rule. The scent of olive trees carried on the breeze mingled now with only silence. Elias contemplated how ideas are far more resilient than empires in this silence. Alexander's Hellenistic culture survived where his political might did not, sowing seeds for future Western and Middle Eastern civilizations to grow.

A few tourists approached, their guide gesturing widely as he explained the site's historical significance. Elias listened from a distance, his eyes squinting against the setting sun, which seemed to set fire to the horizon. How many leaders today face dilemmas similar to those of Alexander? How many modern corporate or otherwise empires are built on precarious grounds without considering succession or legacy?

As dusk settled over Pella, ending another day's exploration into history's vast corridors, Elias couldn't help but wonder: What indeed remains when all else has fallen away?

The Echoes of a Conquered World

When Alexander the Great breathed his last in the palace of Nebuchadnezzar II in Babylon, he left behind not just an empire that stretched from Greece to India but also a legacy shaped by a mosaic of cultures and ideas. His premature death at the tender age of 32 plunged his expansive realm into chaos as his generals, the Diadochi, scrambled for control, leading to the eventual fragmentation of his empire. Yet, despite this political disintegration, Alexander's influence permeated through the ages, proving that ideas can indeed be indomitable.

Alexander's lack of a clear succession plan is often cited as a critical oversight that precipitated the collapse of his territorial acquisitions. *This chapter delves into the immediate aftermath* of his demise, examining how this oversight set the stage for the ensuing wars among his successors, which reshaped the ancient world's political landscape. The narrative we explore here concerns loss, adaptation, and enduring influence.

The cultural and political ideologies Alexander championed continued to thrive long after the territories were divided. His vision of homonoia, or brotherhood among people, although idealistic, seeded the early concepts of a Hellenistic culture that blended diverse customs and traditions across continents. This chapter explores how these seeds grew into lasting influences that persisted well beyond the lifespans of their initial cultivators.

Moreover, Alexander's story is a testament to how personal charisma and visionary leadership can imprint on history in ways that physical boundaries and political structures cannot confine. As we dissect how Alexander's personality cult influenced administrative practices and cultural integration across his empire, it becomes evident that ***his leadership style became a blueprint*** for many who came after him.

Through this introspective exploration, we aim to understand the tangible and intangible remnants of Alexander's conquests. How did his approach to governance and cultural assimilation inform future empires? How did his exploits inspire both conquests and connections across diverse cultures?

Reflecting on these themes offers broader lessons about the power of visionary leadership and cultural openness in shaping civilizations. It also suggests what modern leaders can learn from Alexander's successes and failures.

Thus, while empires may crumble under the weight of their expanse, as did Alexander's, ***the ideas that fuel them can endure***, influencing far-reaching corners of human civilization. This chapter invites readers to look beyond mere historical events to understand how powerful ideas traverse through time and space, much like the enduring legacy of a young Macedonian king who once dreamt of conquering the world.

Alexander's premature death at 32 left a significant void in his empire, primarily due to the absence of a clear succession plan.

This lack of foresight on Alexander's part ultimately led to the disintegration of his vast empire as ambitious generals vied for power and control over different regions. The consequences of this power struggle were profound, resulting in the fragmentation of the once-unified empire into several warring factions. ***The absence of a strong leader to succeed Alexander created a power vacuum that set the stage for years of conflict and instability.***

As Alexander's generals, known as the Diadochi, grappled for supremacy, they divided his conquests amongst themselves, establishing separate kingdoms in Egypt, Asia Minor, and beyond. This division weakened the centralized authority that had characterized

Alexander's rule, leading to internal strife and external threats from neighboring powers. *The failure to secure a smooth transition of power not only jeopardized the empire's stability but also sowed seeds of discord that would persist for generations.*

The repercussions of Alexander's untimely demise reverberated throughout his empire, highlighting the importance of succession planning in maintaining political stability and continuity. *His failure to designate an apparent heir or establish a robust system for transferring power underscored the fragility of empires built on individual charisma and military prowess alone.* The chaos following his death is a cautionary tale about the perils of neglecting long-term governance in favor of short-term conquest.

Despite the disintegration of Alexander's empire into rival factions, his legacy endured through the cultural and political influences he had imparted to the regions he had conquered. **While his empire crumbled, his ideas and practices continued to shape the societies that emerged from its ruins, demonstrating the lasting impact of visionary leadership even in times of upheaval.** The aftermath of Alexander's death is a poignant reminder that empires may fall. Still, the legacies they leave behind can endure far beyond their physical boundaries.

Please continue reading to explore how Alexander's cultural and political ideas persisted despite the fracturing of his empire.

Despite the fragmentation of Alexander the Great's empire after his untimely death, his cultural and political ideas continued to resonate across the lands he once conquered. The impact of Alexander's legacy was not confined by geographical boundaries but transcended them, leaving a lasting imprint on the societies that succeeded his rule. *His vision of a Hellenistic world, where Greek culture intertwined with local traditions, persisted long after his empire crumbled.* The fusion of Greek philosophy, art, and language with diverse cultures created a rich tapestry that endured beyond the disintegration of his conquests.

The spread of Greek ideas and customs under Alexander's reign fostered cultural exchange and intellectual growth in regions far beyond Greece. This cultural diffusion led to new artistic styles, architectural achievements, and philosophical dialogues that shaped civilizations for centuries. *The enduring legacy of this amalgamation of cultures is evident in the art, literature, and architecture of regions once under Alexander's sway,* showcasing a blend of influences that continue to captivate scholars and enthusiasts alike.

Alexander's political ideals also left a profound mark on subsequent rulers, inspiring them to emulate his strategies and governance methods. His belief in meritocracy, centralized rule, and strategic military tactics influenced leaders who sought to establish powerful empires in his wake. *The concept of a universal empire governed by a strong central authority became a model for ambitious conquerors who followed in Alexander's footsteps,* shaping the course of history in ways unforeseen by the young king himself.

The legacy of Alexander's empire was not solely confined to political and cultural realms but extended to philosophical and scientific advancements. The flourishing of knowledge in mathematics, astronomy, and medicine owed much to the interconnected world that Alexander had forged through his conquests. Scholars from diverse backgrounds converged in centers of learning established by Alexander, exchanging ideas and discoveries that laid the foundation for future scientific breakthroughs.

Despite the dissolution of his empire, Alexander's legacy endured through the preservation and dissemination of knowledge across borders, transcending linguistic barriers and ideological differences. The libraries he founded became beacons of wisdom for generations seeking enlightenment and education. *The spirit of intellectual curiosity fostered by Alexander's patronage continued to inspire scholars to push the boundaries of human understanding,* ensuring that his influence would persist long after his empire had faded into history.

As we reflect on the lasting impact of Alexander's cultural and political ideas despite the demise of his empire, we are reminded that *the power of visionary leadership transcends mere conquests or territorial boundaries.* It is in the enduring legacy of ideas, in the fusion of diverse cultures, and in the pursuit of knowledge that true greatness resides, immortalizing those who dare to dream beyond their lifetimes. In embracing these legacies, we inherit not just history but a blueprint for shaping a better future—a future where innovation, inclusivity, and intellectual curiosity reign supreme.

Discussing the Enduring Legacy

As empires rise and fall, ideas and cultural influences often outlast political entities. In the case of Alexander the Great, his legacy endured long after his empire fragmented. *Despite the disintegration of his conquests, the impact of Alexander's cultural and political ideas continued to shape future generations*. The fusion of Greek and Eastern cultures during his rule left a lasting imprint on art, architecture, philosophy, and language.

Alexander's influence spread far and wide through disseminating knowledge in fields such as science, mathematics, and medicine. The famous Library of Alexandria, founded in Egypt during his reign, became a beacon of intellectual advancement for centuries.

Scholars from various backgrounds gathered there to share ideas and push the boundaries of human understanding.

The concept of Hellenism, the spread of Greek culture throughout the lands conquered by Alexander, paved the way for a new era of learning and innovation. *Blending diverse traditions with Greek ideals created a rich tapestry of knowledge transcending borders.*

This cultural exchange fostered an environment where creativity thrived, leading to advancements in literature, art, and science that have reverberated throughout time.

Even as political entities crumbled, the enduring legacy of Alexander's vision for a unified world inspired future leaders. The idea of a global community where different cultures could coexist and thrive gained traction in various empires that rose after his downfall. ***His dream of unity through diversity resonated with leaders seeking to bridge divides and foster cooperation.***

While Alexander's empire may have fractured upon his untimely death, his legacy remained unbroken. ***His impact on culture, politics, and intellectual pursuits endured through the ages***, serving as a testament to the power of ideas to transcend the passage of time. As we reflect on history, it becomes evident that true greatness lies not only in conquest but in the enduring influence one leaves on the world long after they are gone.

In the wake of Alexander the Great's untimely demise at 32, a gaping void was left where a robust succession plan should have been. This oversight did not merely stir political turmoil; it fractured a burgeoning empire. Yet, as we've explored, the dissolution of his territorial reign did not spell the end of Alexander's influence. His vision—a cocktail of cultural integration and political innovation—permeates modern society.

Step 1: Assessing the Consequences of Alexander's Lack of a Succession Plan

Our journey through Alexander's legacy begins with the stark ramifications of his absence of an apparent heir. The immediate aftermath was characterized by fierce power struggles and a fragmented realm, where once unity was under his command. This first step isn't just about understanding the political upheaval but recognizing how these events set the stage for the enduring aspects of his legacy.

***Step 2: Exploring the Continued Influence of Alexander's
Cultural and Political Ideas***

Next, we delve into how Alexander's ideals survived the wreckage of his empire. His policies on cultural assimilation fostered an environment where diverse customs and beliefs could intermingle, laying the groundwork for a more interconnected world. This exploration isn't merely academic—it's about seeing the threads of his influence woven into the fabric of subsequent civilizations and recognizing the blueprint he laid for cultural cohesion.

***Step 3: Discussing How Ideas and Cultural Influences Can
Endure***

Our final contemplation circles back to the resilience of ideas. Alexander's vision transcends the collapse of his empire, echoing through the ages. This enduring impact underscores a profound truth: while empires are mortal, ideas are immortal. It's here we understand that the seeds planted by visionary leaders can bloom long after their departure, influencing countless generations.

This structured approach—starting with the consequences of Alexander's oversight, examining his lasting cultural impact, and understanding the longevity of ideas—helps us appreciate how his legacy continues to shape our world. Each step builds on the last, illustrating historical events and their long-term implications.

As we reflect on Alexander's story, it becomes clear that his actual conquest was not through territory but through enduring ideas that continue to inspire and influence. This is a poignant reminder of how leadership can echo through eternity—not through dominion but through vision and influence. Thus, even as we read this chapter, Alexander's legacy invites us to ponder the lasting power of ideas and their indelible marks on human history.

Chapter 5: Timeless Themes: Ambition, Leadership, and Unity

When Ambition Meets the Reality of Leadership

The sun hung low over the bustling market square, casting long shadows that stretched like fingers across the cobblestones. Amidst the hum of activity, Thomas, a young entrepreneur with dreams as vast as the empire Alexander once commanded, navigated through the crowd. His mind buzzed with thoughts of his recent business venture—a daring attempt to merge cultures in his new line of products, inspired by his admiration for Alexander's strategy of cultural integration.

As he passed stalls flaunting spices from distant lands and fabrics woven with intricate designs, Thomas reflected on how Alexander would have felt, stepping into a foreign land with the ambition to unite rather than conquer. The scent of cinnamon and saffron filled the air, mingling with the sound of diverse languages that reminded him of his team—people he chose not because they were alike but because they were different.

Thomas stopped momentarily to watch a potter, her hands skillfully shaping clay into a beautiful vase. He thought about his role as a leader. Was he shaping his team effectively? Were his ambitions blinding him to their needs and potential? Leadership was more than just directing; it was understanding each unique individual.

The potter knew her clay; did he know his people? Thomas realized that understanding his team members' strengths, weaknesses, and motivations was crucial to effective leadership.

His phone rang—a call from his business partner Lydia, no doubt about their next big meeting. As he answered, he caught sight of himself in a shop window. The reflection showed a man determined yet fraught with doubts, much like Alexander might have been when faced with revolts or exhaustion among his ranks.

They spoke briefly about strategies and goals, but hanging up left Thomas feeling more isolated in his quest. Was he leading or merely pushing forward? Did integrating cultures mean losing one's identity or finding new ones together? The challenges of cultural integration in business, such as language barriers and differing work styles, were not lost on Thomas. He knew that successful integration required patience, understanding, and a willingness to adapt.

As evening drew near and the market slowly emptied, Thomas observed an old man pack up unsold goods—remnants of effort unseen by most but meaningful to those who understood value beyond mere currency.

He walked home pondering not just on profits and expansion but on legacy and fulfillment. What did success indeed mean if it came at the cost of connection? Thomas understood that in his pursuit of success, he had to balance personal achievements with maintaining meaningful connections with his team and partners. This balance, he realized, was an essential aspect of effective leadership.

Was it possible that Alexander's true greatness lay not in the lands he conquered but in the cultural bridges he attempted to build?

Unveiling the Timeless: What Alexander the Great Teaches Us About Today's World

The story of Alexander the Great is not just a tale from ancient history but a source of valuable lessons for today's leaders. Despite being over two millennia old, his strategies and visions are remarkably relevant to contemporary business, governance, and community-building challenges. This chapter explores how Alexander's timeless themes can inform and inspire current and future generations in their leadership roles.

Alexander's relentless ambition is a beacon for anyone who aspires to transcend ordinary boundaries. In exploring his journey, we traverse the vast expanses he conquered and uncover the internal drive that propelled him beyond known worlds. His example prompts us to reflect on our ambitions and our pursuits in our careers and lives. It compels us to ask: What are our conquests?

Does mere personal gain mark them, or do they contribute to a larger good?

Leadership under Alexander was marked by authority, foresight, and inclusivity. His ability to lead a diverse group toward a common goal offers rich insights for today's leaders in multicultural environments. Whether helping a startup, managing a multinational corporation, or leading a community initiative, understanding Alexander's leadership style can shed light on managing diverse teams effectively while fostering an environment of mutual respect and collaboration. This understanding can empower you to navigate the complexities of multicultural leadership with confidence and grace.

Moreover, Alexander's approach to cultural integration—merging differing customs and ideals into a unified empire—resonates with today's globalized interactions. His policies not only promoted tolerance but also embraced cultural diversity, enriching the fabric of his empire. This aspect of his rule offers valuable perspectives on navigating today's culturally complex business and social landscapes.

Visionary leadership and *strategic thinking* were hallmarks of Alexander's success. These qualities are indispensable in contemporary settings where rapid change and unpredictability is the norm. By studying his strategies, modern leaders can glean insights into long-term planning with flexibility, balancing bold visions with the practicalities of day-to-day execution.

This chapter aims to bridge millennia by linking ancient successes with modern scenarios. By examining Alexander's life, we pay homage to his historical significance and extract practical applications for today's world. It invites readers to reflect on their leadership styles, ambitions, and methods of cultural engagement, inspiring them to apply these age-old principles in their modern contexts and enhance their approaches to leadership and community building today.

Understanding how these age-old principles apply in modern contexts can enhance our leadership and community-building approaches today. Each section of this chapter will highlight aspects of Alexander's rule and connect these elements with contemporary examples that resonate with young entrepreneurs and seasoned leaders alike.

Thus, as we explore ambition, leadership, and unity in the context of Alexander the Great's life, we uncover historical facts and living truths relevant to our times. These lessons encourage us to think bigger, act wiser, and unite more broadly in various spheres of influence.

Ambition and leadership are timeless themes that resonate across centuries, transcending the boundaries of historical eras. Alexander the Great's ambition to conquer the known world and his exceptional leadership abilities continue to inspire individuals in modern-day personal and professional scenarios. His unwavering determination to achieve greatness is a beacon for those striving for success.

Alexander's relentless pursuit of his goals can be a source of motivation for anyone facing challenges or setbacks. In personal growth or career aspirations, channeling his ambitious spirit can propel individuals to surpass their limitations and reach new heights, inspiring them to strive for greatness in their own lives.

Leadership lessons from Alexander's life can offer valuable insights into effective management and decision-making. His ability to inspire loyalty and commitment among his followers highlights the importance of strong leadership in achieving collective goals. In contemporary workplaces, leaders can learn from Alexander's approach to fostering a sense of unity and purpose within their teams. Individuals can cultivate a culture of collaboration, innovation, and excellence by emulating their leadership style.

The connection between Alexander's ambition and leadership qualities extends beyond individual aspirations to broader societal contexts. In today's fast-paced and competitive world, ambitious leaders are often at the forefront of driving change and progress. By embracing ambitious goals and leading with vision, individuals can shape the future landscape of their industries and communities. *Alexander's legacy serves as a reminder that bold leadership is essential for navigating complex challenges and seizing growth opportunities.*

Continue reading to explore how Alexander's efforts at cultural integration are mirrored in contemporary settings.

In examining how Alexander the Great's efforts at cultural integration resonate in contemporary settings, we can draw parallels to the importance of embracing diversity and fostering inclusivity in today's world. *Cultural integration* is not just about coexistence but about truly understanding and appreciating different customs, beliefs, and perspectives. In a globalized society where interactions between various cultures are inevitable, bridging differences and finding common ground becomes paramount.

Alexander's approach to cultural integration was marked by a genuine curiosity about the customs and traditions of his conquered lands. He didn't seek to impose his own culture but instead embraced the diversity he encountered, incorporating elements from different societies into his empire. This open-mindedness and willingness to learn from others can be emulated in modern times.

Businesses, organizations, and communities benefit greatly from *embracing cultural diversity* in contemporary settings. This fosters an inclusive environment where individuals from different backgrounds feel valued and respected, which in turn fosters creativity and innovation. Just as Alexander's empire prospered through cultural exchange, modern-day institutions can achieve success by leveraging the unique strengths that diverse perspectives bring.

Moreover, in a world where ***global interconnectedness*** is increasingly evident, understanding and respecting cultural differences are essential for peaceful coexistence. By learning from Alexander's example of embracing diversity rather than seeing it as a threat, we can work towards building a more harmonious society where unity is celebrated and divisions are bridged.

Leaders who prioritize cultural integration demonstrate visionary thinking and strategic foresight. They understand that harnessing the richness of diverse backgrounds leads to stronger teams, better decision-making processes, and, ultimately, more sustainable success. By recognizing the value of inclusivity and actively promoting cross-cultural understanding, leaders can create environments where every voice is heard and every perspective is considered.

In conclusion, Alexander the Great's legacy extends beyond military conquests to encompass profound lessons in cultural integration that remain relevant today. By acknowledging the importance of embracing diversity, fostering inclusivity, and promoting unity across cultures, individuals and organizations can strive towards a more interconnected world where mutual respect and cooperation prevail.

In today's fast-paced and ever-changing world, visionary leadership and strategic thinking are crucial for success in various fields.

Drawing parallels from Alexander the Great's life, we can glean valuable insights into these critical qualities that are timeless and applicable in modern times. ***Alexander's visionary leadership*** was characterized by his ability to see beyond the immediate circumstances and envision a grander future, much like successful leaders today, who possess the foresight to anticipate trends and navigate challenges proactively.

Strategic thinking, a cornerstone of Alexander's conquests, involved meticulous planning, adaptability to changing situations, and a deep understanding of his resources and surroundings. This strategic mindset is just as relevant today as it was in ancient times.

Leaders who can analyze complex situations, make informed decisions, and pivot when necessary are better equipped to steer their organizations toward success amidst uncertainty.

Embracing ***visionary leadership*** means setting ambitious yet achievable goals that inspire others to follow suit. Alexander's audacious campaigns across continents exemplify this quality, pushing the boundaries of what was thought possible at the time.

Similarly, modern leaders who dare to dream big, challenge the status quo, and rally their teams behind a shared vision often achieve remarkable feats that seemed unattainable initially.

On the other hand, strategic thinking involves breaking down overarching goals into actionable steps, assessing risks and opportunities, and making calculated moves toward the desired outcome. By learning from Alexander's strategic prowess in battle and diplomacy, contemporary leaders can cultivate a mindset that balances long-term vision with practical execution, ensuring sustainable growth and success for their endeavors.

In today's interconnected world, where global collaboration is increasingly vital, ***Alexander's efforts at cultural integration offer*** profound lessons for leaders seeking to bridge divides and foster unity among diverse groups. His ability to blend Greek and Eastern customs while respecting local traditions paved the way for a harmonious coexistence that transcended cultural barriers.

Likewise, modern leaders who embrace diversity, promote inclusivity, and cultivate an environment of mutual respect can harness the collective strengths of multicultural teams to achieve remarkable outcomes.

By reflecting on Alexander's legacy of ambition, leadership, and cross-cultural engagement, we can distill timeless principles that resonate with contemporary challenges. As we navigate the complexities of the modern world, embodying visionary leadership traits such as foresight, courage, and empathy can guide us toward achieving our ambitions while fostering unity among diverse communities. Strategic thinking and an openness to cultural integration enable us to adapt to changing landscapes and seize opportunities for growth and collaboration in an ever-evolving global landscape.

As we reflect on Alexander the Great's life, it becomes increasingly clear how his stories of ambition, leadership, and cultural integration are not just relics of the past but vital lessons for our present and future. His drive to achieve and visionary leadership style blueprints modern personal and professional growth. In today's fast-paced world, where leadership often seems fragmented, Alexander's example encourages a more unified and strategic approach.

His efforts to blend diverse cultures under his rule mirror the globalized interactions we navigate daily in business and social settings. This aspect of his leadership shows us the value of embracing diversity and fostering inclusivity, principles that are fundamental to contemporary organizational success and societal harmony.

Moreover, the strategic thinking that marked Alexander's campaigns—the foresight, the planning, and the execution—parallels the visionary leadership needed in today's complex digital landscapes. Whether we are leading a team, managing a project, or steering a company, the principles of clear vision and steadfast purpose remain unchanged.

Reflecting on these themes, we find historical insights and personal guidance. The ambition that propelled Alexander can inspire us to set higher goals and reach beyond our current grasp. His leadership style, marked by both boldness and unity, can serve as a model for leading with integrity and empathy. And his approach to cultural integration can teach us the importance of respecting and valuing diverse perspectives in our interconnected world.

Let these timeless themes motivate us to excel in our endeavors and to lead with courage and wisdom. Like Alexander, may we also leave a legacy that stands the test of time, not through conquests but through our positive impact on those around us. Let's carry forward the lessons from his life as we navigate the complexities of our own, striving always to blend ambition with moral leadership and cultural respect.

Chapter 6: Cultural Melting Pots: Then and Now

Amidst the Echoes of Ancient Cultures

In the heart of a bustling modern city, with its skyscrapers clawing at the sky and streets buzzing with a mosaic of languages, Samira, a cultural integration officer, navigated through the crowded sidewalks. Her role involved fostering understanding and collaboration among diverse communities—much like Alexander's ancient policies aimed at blending disparate cultures under one empire.

As she walked past food stalls releasing steam into the cool air, each aroma seemed to carry tales from different corners of the world. The scents mingled in a dance as old as time itself, reminding her of how Alexander's cities must have thrived as centers of cultural fusion. She pondered how this historical precedent could guide her current project: creating a festival to celebrate the city's diverse heritage while promoting unity.

Samira stopped by a small park tucked away between two old buildings. Children played in harmony, their laughter cutting through the urban noise—a vivid tableau of living diversity. She watched them momentarily, thinking about how these children represented what she aimed to achieve on a larger scale: seamless integration where differences were celebrated rather than tolerated.

Inside a nearby café, she ordered coffee. She settled by a window overlooking an intersection crowded with people from all walks of life. With each sip, her mind wandered back to Alexander's strategies—how he conquered lands and hearts by encouraging his soldiers to marry locals and adopt local customs. Could similar principles be adapted to modern urban policies? Could cultural respect and integration be fostered through shared community activities?

As Samira scribbled notes in her journal, blending historical insights with contemporary initiatives, she felt anchored by the weight of history yet buoyed by possibilities for the future. Was it possible that solutions to today's challenges in multicultural interaction lay hidden within ancient practices? Could we learn from Alexander's vision to enhance our approach towards global multiculturalism today?

Bridging Ancient Ambitions with Modern Mosaics

When we delve into the annals of history, Alexander the Great emerges as a formidable conqueror and a visionary in cultural integration. His legacy, often overshadowed by his military exploits, includes the profound impact of his policies on governance and multicultural coexistence. As we explore the echoes of Alexander's strategies in contemporary global dynamics, we discover invaluable lessons on unity amid diversity.

A Historical Blueprint for Today's Global Cities

Alexander's establishment of cities across his empire was a strategic move aimed at more than mere political control; it was a deliberate effort to *cultivate cultural convergence*. These cities, from Alexandria in Egypt to Ai-Khanoum in what is now Afghanistan, were not just administrative centers but vibrant hubs where people and traditions from diverse backgrounds intermingled and influenced one another. This historical scenario mirrors today's global cities like New York, London, and Dubai, where multifaceted cultures blend seamlessly.

The Double-Edged Sword of Multiculturalism

The benefits of multicultural societies are manifold—innovation, creativity, and a broader societal perspective. However, these societies face significant challenges, such as social fragmentation and conflict. By reflecting on how Alexander managed these issues—promoting Hellenistic culture while respecting local traditions—we gain insights into managing modern multicultural conflicts. This historical perspective provides us with examples of the strength of diversity and the tensions that can arise from it.

Governance That Transcends Time

Alexander's approach to governance was revolutionary; his policies promoted inclusivity and integration among conquered peoples. He respected and embraced local customs and religions, incorporating them into his empire's administration and daily life.

This strategy fostered loyalty and stability among diverse groups—a lesson that resonates powerfully in today's globalized society, where governance often struggles to balance unity and diversity.

This chapter will traverse these historical corridors to understand how Alexander's ancient policies provide a framework for addressing contemporary challenges in multicultural interactions.

We will explore how his foresight in creating inclusive administrative frameworks offers lessons for today's leaders in fostering cohesive societies amidst cultural diversity.

This exploration is not merely an academic exercise; it is a journey toward understanding how the past informs our present and guides our future in navigating the complexities of global multiculturalism. By studying Alexander's strategies, we can better appreciate the intricate tapestry of cultures that shape our modern world.

Through this reflective journey, we aim to inspire readers to embrace the rich diversity that defines human civilization, encouraging a deeper appreciation for the ancient roots of contemporary global interactions. This chapter promises to be a compelling narrative that connects the dots across millennia, highlighting how historical strategies can illuminate solutions to modern challenges.

Alexander the Great's vision for culturally diverse cities was revolutionary in ancient times. He founded cities like Alexandria in Egypt, where Greek, Egyptian, Persian, and other cultures intermingled, creating a melting pot of traditions, languages, and beliefs. These cities were hubs of trade, knowledge exchange, and cultural diffusion. Fast forward to today, and we see a similar phenomenon in global cities like New York, London, and Dubai.

These modern metropolises are akin to Alexander's multicultural cities, where people from all over the world converge, bringing their unique identities and perspectives to create vibrant urban tapestries.

The parallels between Alexander's ancient cities and today's global cities are striking. Both serve as beacons of diversity and tolerance, where individuals from different backgrounds coexist harmoniously. *They are centers of innovation and creativity*, where cross-cultural pollination leads to new ideas and ways of thinking. Just as Alexander's cities benefited from exchanging goods and knowledge along the Silk Road, modern global towns thrive on the flow of information, technology, and capital across borders.

However, with cultural diversity comes its own set of challenges.

Navigating cultural differences in ancient and modern contexts *requires empathy,* understanding, and a willingness to embrace the unfamiliar. Misunderstandings can arise when diverse cultures clash or when prejudices cloud interactions. *Building bridges between cultures requires active participation*, dialogue, and a commitment to fostering inclusivity.

Despite the challenges, *multicultural societies' beauty lies in their ability to celebrate differences* while finding common ground.

Alexander's legacy of establishing culturally diverse cities is a testament to the enduring value of embracing diversity. Today's global cities continue this legacy by showcasing the richness that arises from cultural fusion.

Are you curious about how these multicultural societies have historically evolved? Let's delve deeper into the benefits and challenges faced by these diverse communities throughout history.

Multicultural societies have historically offered many benefits, enriching the tapestry of human experience with diverse perspectives, traditions, and innovations. *Cultural exchange fosters* creativity and understanding, leading to new ideas and advancements that might not have been possible in a homogenous society. Exposure to different ways of life promotes *tolerance* and *empathy*, breaking down barriers and fostering a sense of global citizenship. *Historically*, multicultural societies have been centers of trade, where ideas and goods flow freely, contributing to economic growth and prosperity for all involved.

However, alongside these benefits come inevitable challenges. *Cultural clashes* can arise from differing beliefs, customs, or values, leading to misunderstandings or conflicts within a multicultural society. *Prejudice* and *discrimination* may rear their ugly heads as fear of the unknown or the *"other"* takes hold.

Language barriers can also hinder effective communication and integration, hindering collaboration and unity within a diverse community. These challenges are not insurmountable but require *open-mindedness, education*, and *dialogue*.

In contemporary times, multicultural societies face similar dynamics but on a global scale. The interconnected world we live in today allows for unprecedented *cultural exchange* and *interaction*, leading to vibrant multicultural communities in major cities worldwide. The benefits of these interactions are evident in the rich tapestry of experiences, cuisines, art forms, and ideas that flourish in such environments. However, challenges persist as well, with issues like *racial tensions, xenophobia*, and *inequality* highlighting the work still needed to achieve true harmony in multicultural settings.

Navigating these complexities requires a delicate balance of *respect, understanding*, and *flexibility* from all members of society. Embracing diversity while fostering a sense of unity is critical to reaping the total rewards of multiculturalism while mitigating its challenges. As we reflect on Alexander's visionary approach to cultural integration within his empire, we can draw parallels to our present-day struggles and triumphs in building harmonious multicultural societies that celebrate our differences while uniting us in our shared humanity.

Analytical Framework

The framework we will explore delves into the comparison between Alexander's establishment of culturally diverse cities and today's global cities. It encompasses several vital dimensions: *cultural integration, governance policies, economic impacts*, and *socio-political challenges*. Each dimension will provide an overview of how Alexander fostered integration through marriages, adopted local customs, and created cultural exchange hubs. This will be compared with modern multicultural policies, economic globalization, and the integration of diverse populations in today's cities. Specific metrics like cultural diversity indices and economic diversity scores will be used to quantify the level of multiculturalism and its effects, offering a systematic approach to understanding the benefits and challenges of multicultural societies.

Cultural Integration

Cultural integration examines how different cultures interact within a society. In Alexander's time, he encouraged his soldiers to marry local women, blending traditions and customs. Similarly, modern global cities witness a fusion of cultures through migration and globalization. The diversity index measures the cultural exchange level, reflecting the variety of ethnicities, languages, and traditions coexisting within a city.

Governance Policies

Governance policies play a crucial role in managing multicultural societies. Alexander implemented inclusive policies that allowed for the coexistence of various cultures under his empire. Today, global cities have policies promoting diversity, inclusion, and equality to ensure harmonious community interactions. These policies are essential for fostering social cohesion and preventing conflicts based on cultural differences.

Economic Impacts

Economic impacts assess how multiculturalism influences the economy of a city or empire. Alexander's diverse cities benefited from trade routes that connected different regions, stimulating economic growth. Economic globalization has increased trade, innovation, and cultural exchange in contemporary global cities. Economic diversity scores measure the economic vibrancy resulting from multicultural interactions.

Socio-Political Challenges

Socio-political challenges examine the issues arising from cultural diversity within a society. In Alexander's empire, tensions sometimes occurred due to cultural differences among conquered peoples. Similarly, modern global cities face challenges such as discrimination, inequality, and social segregation based on ethnicity or religion. Addressing these challenges requires proactive policies that promote social harmony and inclusivity.

Understanding these dimensions provides insight into how historical approaches to cultural integration can inform present-day multicultural dynamics. By analyzing these components through a historical lens and applying them to contemporary contexts, we gain a deeper understanding of the complexities and opportunities presented by multicultural societies.

Reflecting on the intricate tapestry of cultures that Alexander the Great wove into the fabric of his empire, it's clear that the seeds of modern multiculturalism were sown long before our time. Through establishing culturally diverse cities, Alexander conquered lands and pioneered a form of governance that celebrated and integrated many ethnic backgrounds, much like the global cities we navigate today.

Both ancient and contemporary multicultural societies offer profound benefits such as increased creativity, broader perspectives, and a richer cultural landscape. Yet, they also present challenges, including social tensions and the complexities of governance across diverse groups. The historical lens through which we view Alexander's strategies reveals that these challenges are manageable. Instead, they are opportunities for growth and innovation.

Alexander's policies echo in today's global interactions. His approach to governance—marked by an openness to diverse cultures and ideas—encourages us to embrace similar inclusivity in our societies. This perspective enriches our communal environments and enhances diplomatic relations and global cooperation.

This exploration reminds us of the timeless nature of certain leadership qualities, such as adaptability, vision, and inclusiveness.

Alexander's life teaches us that a society's strength lies not just in its military might but also in its cultural richness and the harmonious coexistence of its people.

As we move forward, let us carry the wisdom from past and present multicultural dynamics. Let's strive to foster environments where diverse voices are heard and integral to decision-making. By doing so, we honor the legacy of leaders like Alexander and take active steps toward crafting a more inclusive world.

May this reflection inspire you to look at your community and its diverse tapestry with renewed appreciation and proactive engagement. Embrace the complexity as an opportunity to build a richer, more vibrant society. After all, in the beautiful mosaic of humanity, every piece is essential.

Chapter 7: Breaking Misconceptions: The Sage Beyond the Soldier

Can the True Measure of a Leader be Found Not in Their Conquests, but in Their Governance?

In the lush valley of the Indus, where the air was thick with the scent of jasmine and the bustling sounds of a market in full swing, Alexander stood, cloaked not just in his typical armor but in contemplation. His eyes surveyed the vibrant tapestry of cultures mingling before him, merchants from far-off lands bartering with local villagers. This was not merely a place of trade but a crucible of cultures, much like his vast empire.

His mind wandered back to the recent councils, where he had passionately argued for policies that would integrate rather than subjugate the newly conquered cities. He remembered how his generals had scoffed at these notions, their minds fixed on loot and tribute rather than lasting peace. Alexander felt a stirring within him, a desire to prove that true power lay in unity and sustainability, not merely conquest.

A young boy darted through the crowd, chasing a runaway goat. Alexander's lips curved into a smile at the simple joy of the child's laughter. This momentary distraction brought him back from his reverie to the sounds around him—the calls of vendors selling spices and textiles to passersby. Each voice carried an undertone of harmony that resonated with Alexander's vision for his empire: diverse yet unified under shared governance.

As he walked through his newly acquired city, ideas formed like soldiers lining up for battle. He could establish schools that taught Greek philosophy and local wisdom. Would it be possible to create civic centers where people could gather to discuss issues pertinent to their community? The challenge was monumental, yet Alexander felt invigorated by it. Each step he took through this city pulsed with potential—a new kind of conquest fought on the grounds of intellect and cultural exchange rather than sheer might.

The sun dipped below the horizon, casting long shadows over the stone paths wound through the marketplace. The air cooled slightly, carrying whispers from one stall to another as people began packing away their goods for the day. Alexander pondered what legacy he wished to leave behind, This momentary calmness enveloped him like evening mist over a battlefield after combat had ceased.

Would future generations remember him only as a conqueror or ruler who sought deeper connections among disparate peoples?

Unveiling Alexander: The Master of Integration, Not Just Conquest

Alexander the Great: a name that resonates through the annals of history as a symbol of conquest and military prowess. Yet, the typical portrayal of Alexander as merely a bold conqueror overshadows his equally significant achievements in governance and cultural integration. This chapter aims to shed light on these lesser-known aspects of his leadership, offering a more nuanced view of his legacy beyond the battlefield.

Revisiting the Realm of Governance

Alexander's approach to governance was revolutionary for his time. Far from being a tyrant who imposed Macedonian customs on conquered territories, he was a pioneering leader who embraced local customs and administrations. This chapter delves into how Alexander respected and integrated diverse cultures within his empire, which was crucial for its sustainability. His policies promoted inclusivity and stability, contradicting the typical image of him as merely a conqueror.

Strategic Accomplishments Beyond Battle

While his military strategies are well-documented and celebrated, Alexander's strategic accomplishments in administration and policy-making are often overlooked. By focusing on these aspects, we understand why his empire, sprawling from Greece to India, remained cohesive despite its vast diversity. His foresight in infrastructure development and urban planning played pivotal roles in enhancing his empire's economic viability and connectivity.

Correcting Historical Oversights

Many historical accounts simplify Alexander's achievements to mere conquests. Still, this narrative does justice to his visionary leadership in areas like law, economy, and culture. By emphasizing these facets, we correct common misconceptions about Alexander and appreciate his efforts toward creating an integrated and sustainable empire.

In exploring these themes, we invite readers to look at Alexander through a lens that highlights his multifaceted contributions to world history. His strategic insight in war and peace positions him as a military commander and a profound sage whose policies laid the groundwork for modern governance concepts.

This chapter is not just about revising history but enriching our understanding of a figure who shaped civilizations by blending rather than dividing them. Through this exploration, we aim to inspire readers to appreciate the complexity and foresight of Alexander's leadership—a testament to his enduring legacy in world history.

Engaging with this content gives one a renewed perspective on Alexander the Great. He is seen as a leader whose true greatness lay as much in his capacity for integration and policy-making as in his battlefield tactics. Thus, we move beyond traditional narratives to embrace a fuller appreciation of one of history's most influential figures.

Alexander the Great's legacy often centers on his military conquests, but delving into his governance and cultural policies reveals a multifaceted leader beyond the battlefield. While his military campaigns were undeniably impressive, exploring the lesser-known aspects of his rule to appreciate the full scope of his accomplishments is equally crucial.

Alexander's governance strategies extended far beyond mere conquest. He implemented policies integrating diverse cultures within his empire, fostering unity through shared values and practices. His administration was marked by a blend of Greek and Persian customs, showcasing his willingness to adapt and embrace diversity rather than impose a singular culture. This approach facilitated smoother governance and laid the foundation for a more inclusive and harmonious society.

In addition to cultural integration, ***Alexander's focus on sustainability*** set him apart as a visionary leader. He established cities and settlements throughout his empire, strategically placing them to promote trade, communication, and stability. By investing in infrastructure and urban planning, he ensured the long-term viability of his conquests, creating a network that would outlast his reign. This emphasis on building for the future underscores Alexander's commitment to leaving a lasting legacy beyond military triumphs.

Under Alexander's rule, cultural policies were characterized by a blend of innovation and respect for local traditions. He encouraged exchanging ideas between regions, fostering intellectual growth and artistic flourishing. By promoting cultural exchange and collaboration, he created a vibrant environment where creativity thrived, leading to advancements in various fields, from art to philosophy. This open-minded approach enriched the empire culturally and paved the way for future developments in the arts and sciences.

Let's explore how Alexander's strategic accomplishments provide deeper insights into his historical impact.

Focusing on Alexander's strategic accomplishments provides a deeper understanding of his historical impact. Beyond the battlefield, Alexander's vision extended to governance, culture, and integration, showcasing a multifaceted leader whose influence reached far beyond military conquests. By delving into his strategic decisions, we uncover a man driven by the desire for expansion and a keen sense of sustaining and uniting diverse territories under his rule.

Alexander's conquests were not merely about territorial expansion; they were strategic moves to create a vast empire where diverse cultures could coexist and thrive. His ability to blend different customs and traditions into a cohesive whole speaks volumes about his foresight and diplomatic skills. Rather than imposing Greek culture forcefully, he encouraged cultural exchange, paving the way for a rich tapestry of ideas and practices to flourish under his reign.

His strategic prowess went beyond mere military tactics.

Alexander's ability to adapt to changing circumstances, forge alliances with local leaders, and establish administrative structures in conquered territories set him apart as a visionary ruler. He understood the importance of winning hearts and minds, laying the foundation for long-term stability in regions under his control.

Focusing on Alexander's strategic accomplishments gives us insight into his legacy as more than just a conqueror. His emphasis on building cities, promoting trade routes, and fostering communication between distant lands reveals a leader who valued connectivity and exchange. Through these endeavors, he sowed the seeds for future cultural exchanges and intellectual growth that would shape history for centuries.

Understanding Alexander's strategic achievements allows us to appreciate the complexities of empire-building. It was about amassing land and creating a network of interdependent regions united by shared interests and mutual respect. His forward-thinking policies laid the groundwork for future empires to emulate, emphasizing cooperation over coercion and inclusivity over exclusivity.

In exploring Alexander's strategic decisions, we uncover a leader ahead of his time. His emphasis on blending cultures, fostering trade, and promoting intellectual exchange foreshadowed modern notions of globalization and interconnectedness. By studying his methods, we can draw parallels to contemporary challenges and opportunities in our increasingly interconnected world.

By peeling back the layers of Alexander's strategic accomplishments, we reveal a leader whose influence transcended borders and periods. His legacy as a strategist, diplomat, and visionary ruler offers valuable lessons for leaders in any field today. Embracing diversity, fostering collaboration, and thinking beyond immediate gains are just some enduring principles we can learn from the sage beyond the soldier.

Through an in-depth exploration of Alexander's strategic achievements, we move beyond simplistic portrayals of him as merely a warrior king. Instead, we uncover a complex figure whose far-reaching impact on history stemmed from military conquests and his innovative governance and cultural integration approaches.

In reevaluating his legacy through this lens, we gain a more nuanced understanding of one of history's most captivating figures.

Alexander the Great is often remembered solely for his military conquests, overshadowing his efforts in integration and sustainability. However, we can correct misconceptions about his leadership and legacy by highlighting these lesser-known aspects of his reign. *Alexander's strategic vision extended beyond battlefields*, focusing on establishing a cohesive empire through cultural assimilation and administrative reforms. His policies aimed at integrating diverse populations and fostering cooperation among conquered territories, showcasing a commitment to long-term stability rather than mere domination.

One fundamental misconception about Alexander is that he was solely a ruthless conqueror. However, a closer look reveals his dedication to fostering unity and understanding among different cultures. *His promotion of cultural exchange and adoption of Persian customs displayed a nuanced approach to governance*, seeking to create a harmonious blend of East and West within his empire. This cultural integration facilitated administration and promoted tolerance and mutual respect among diverse populations under his rule.

Contrary to popular belief, Alexander's legacy extends far beyond military achievements. His emphasis on sustainable governance and infrastructure development laid the groundwork for future empires to thrive. *By implementing administrative reforms and encouraging local autonomy*, he established a framework for effective governance that outlasted his lifetime. This focus on long-term stability showcases a strategic mindset geared towards ensuring the longevity of his empire.

Another misconception surrounding Alexander is that he neglected his subjects' welfare. In reality, he implemented various social policies to improve the lives of those within his empire.

From promoting education and urban planning to providing economic opportunities, Alexander demonstrated a holistic approach to governance that prioritized the well-being of his people. These initiatives not only enhanced the quality of life for many but also contributed to the overall prosperity of his empire.

It is essential to recognize Alexander's multifaceted contributions beyond military conquests. Acknowledging his integration and sustainability efforts gives us a more comprehensive understanding of his leadership style and historical impact. *His ability to govern with foresight and inclusivity set him apart as a visionary leader* whose influence transcended mere territorial expansion. By highlighting these aspects of his reign, we can see that Alexander was a strategist and statesman who shaped empires through diplomacy and cultural exchange.

In correcting misconceptions about Alexander, we uncover a leader who values unity, diversity, and long-term stability. His approach to governance reflects wisdom beyond mere conquest, emphasizing the importance of cultural integration and sustainable policies. *By delving into these lesser-known facets of his rule*, we can paint a more accurate portrait of Alexander as a ruler who sought power and cohesion among diverse peoples.

Beyond the Battlefield

Alexander the Great is often celebrated as a military genius, but to view him solely through this lens is to miss the richness of his leadership. This chapter has sought to illuminate the lesser-known facets of his governance and cultural initiatives, which were as strategic as his battlefield tactics and crucial for the sustainability of his vast empire.

Governance and cultural policies were far from footnotes in his reign; they were, in fact, central components of Alexander's strategy. His efforts to integrate diverse cultures and implement forward-thinking policies highlight a ruler ahead of his time. By promoting a blend of customs and encouraging marriages between Macedonians and Persians, Alexander wasn't merely conquering new territories but weaving a tapestry of cultures that could stand the test of time.

Strategic accomplishments go beyond mere conquests. They encompass his vision for a unified empire that could thrive on the synergy of its parts. Alexander's foresight in establishing cities like Alexandria as cultural and commercial hubs demonstrates his understanding of power dynamics and economic sustainability.

These cities weren't just military outposts; they were beacons of Hellenistic culture and learning strategically positioned to enhance trade and cultural exchange.

Correcting *common misconceptions* about Alexander involves recognizing his role as a thoughtful leader who valued the integration of the peoples and regions under his rule. While his military conquests cannot be understated, his true genius perhaps lay in his approach to governance—his ability to see beyond the immediacy of battle to the long-term implications of his actions.

Reflecting on Alexander's life, it becomes clear that his historical impact was not merely the result of his battlefield prowess but also his sophisticated approach to rule. He was not just building an empire but laying the foundations for a new world order that valued cultural coexistence and foresaw a future where diverse peoples could contribute to shared prosperity.

By revisiting these aspects of Alexander's rule, we gain a more nuanced understanding of his achievements and valuable insights into leadership that transcends ages. His story encourages us to look beyond surface-level interpretations and appreciate the depth of strategic thinking required to manage such a vast and diverse empire.

As we move forward in this book, let us renew our appreciation for Alexander as a conqueror and a visionary leader whose policies laid down the early groundwork for modern governance and cultural integration. His legacy, viewed through this broader lens, offers timeless lessons on the power of inclusive leadership and strategic foresight.

Chapter 8: Trailblazers of Globalization: Cultural Exchanges and Their Impacts

When Cultures Converge

In the bustling heart of Alexandria, under the warm embrace of a midday sun, merchants from distant lands mingled with scholars and poets. The city birthed from Alexander the Great's ambition, thrived as a melting pot where ideas and goods exchanged hands as freely as the air they breathed. Amidst this vibrant chaos, a young scribe named Darius pondered the profound impacts of such cultural exchanges.

Darius walked through the market, his eyes catching glimpses of silk from the East and spices whose aromas spoke of unseen forests and uncharted paths. He listened intently to conversations around him, snippets about geometry from Greek scholars mingling with Persian tales of heroes and gods. Each step he took wove him deeper into the tapestry of shared human endeavor that Alexander had envisioned.

His mind wandered to his family's narratives; his father was a Persian craftsman who had married a Greek woman. At home, their languages danced in a delicate balance, respecting and enriching each other. This personal blend of cultures mirrored the more significant synthesis happening around him—it was as if Alexander's conquests had torn down invisible walls, allowing armies, hearts, and minds to traverse freely.

Darius paused beside a stall selling Egyptian papyrus, feeling its coarse texture between his fingers. He thought about how this simple item connected scribes worldwide, enabling knowledge to travel vast distances. The stall owner caught his gaze and smiled, offering him a sheet as if he knew Darius's thoughts were on grander things than mere trade.

Could Alexander's actual conquest not be of lands but of human understanding?

Beyond Conquests: The Unseen Threads of Alexander's Empire

When we think of Alexander the Great, images of epic battles and unprecedented conquests often dominate our perceptions. However, a profound narrative unfolded beneath the surface of military campaigns—one of cultural synthesis and global connectivity that presaged modern globalization. Alexander's expeditions across continents did more than expand territories; they bridged diverse civilizations, creating a mosaic of cultural exchange that enriched his empire and the world.

The Role of Conquests in Cultural Exchange

The seeds of cultural integration were sown through Alexander's strategic alliances and settlements across his empire. By founding over seventy cities, he inadvertently laid the groundwork for cultural exchange. These cities became melting pots where Greeks, Persians, Egyptians, and Indians coexisted and collaborated. Markets buzzed with traders from around the world exchanging goods and ideas. This fusion of cultures under Alexander's reign was not incidental but a deliberate outcome of his vision to integrate the diverse peoples within his realm.

Early Globalization and Interconnectedness

Alexander's approach to governance also reflected an early form of globalization. His policy of encouraging marriages between Macedonian soldiers and local women and adopting local customs facilitated a deeper cultural integration that transcended mere political dominion. This blend extended to administrative reforms where local rulers had significant autonomy under the overarching unity of their empire. Such strategies illustrate how interconnectedness was a byproduct and a strategic element in Alexander's rule.

Lasting Impacts on the World

The long-term impacts of these cultural exchanges are monumental. They laid the initial paths for the Silk Roads, enhancing trade between the East and West long after Alexander's death. The Hellenistic period that followed his reign saw a flourishing of science, philosophy, and arts as a direct result of these cross-cultural interactions. The echoes of this cultural amalgamation are evident in the spread of Hellenistic art and thought across Asia and Africa.

By examining these facets, we begin to appreciate Alexander as a military strategist and a visionary who understood the power of culture in binding diverse peoples together. His legacy is not confined to the territories he conquered but is also woven into the rich tapestry of global culture that continues to influence us today.

This exploration of Alexander as a harbinger of globalization offers us fresh insights into his strategies and successes. It encourages us to look beyond the battlefield to understand his profound impact on world history.

In this chapter, we will delve deeper into how these cultural exchanges influenced global history and how they serve as early examples of globalization processes that have shaped our modern world. Through this exploration, we aim to shed light on Alexander's lesser-known role as a facilitator of cultural fusion and global connectivity.

Engaging with this narrative enables us to view historical figures like Alexander through a broader lens, appreciating their contributions beyond conventional achievements. It also inspires us to consider how our interactions with diverse cultures can lead to more prosperous, more interconnected lives. Through these reflections, we connect with history intellectually, emotionally, and socially, drawing lessons that resonate with our contemporary experiences in an increasingly globalized society.

Alexander's conquests were not mere military campaigns but pivotal in fostering cultural discovery and exchange. As he expanded his empire, Alexander actively encouraged sharing ideas, goods, and traditions among diverse civilizations. The Greeks, Egyptians, Persians, and Indians all played a part in this exchange, enriching their cultures while creating a more interconnected world. This early form of globalization laid the groundwork for a world where boundaries blurred and connections between distant lands grew stronger.

The impact of Alexander's conquests went beyond territorial expansion. His vision extended to the cross-pollination of cultures, leading to a melting pot of traditions that influenced his empire's art, architecture, language, and philosophy. The Greeks absorbed knowledge from the East, adopting new practices and beliefs that shaped their society. Meanwhile, the conquered regions embraced Greek culture, creating a fusion that transformed both conquerors and conquerors.

Cultural exchanges during Alexander's reign were not one-sided affairs; instead, they were dynamic interactions where each civilization contributed unique perspectives. The Greeks introduced new artistic techniques and philosophical ideas to the East, while the Persians and Indians shared their rich cultural heritage with the West. This mutual sharing of knowledge led to a flourishing of creativity and innovation that transcended geographical borders.

The interconnectedness fostered by Alexander's conquests paved the way for future generations to build upon this legacy of cultural exchange. Ideas spread like wildfire in this newfound era of connectivity, inspiring advancements in various fields such as science, literature, and governance. The exchange of goods also flourished, with trade routes expanding and merchants traversing vast distances to bring exotic products from distant lands.

The cultural tapestry woven during Alexander's time laid the foundation for a more cosmopolitan world where diversity was tolerated and celebrated. People from different backgrounds interacted freely, learning from one another and creating a richer tapestry of human experience. This era marked a turning point in history where globalization began to take root, setting the stage for future interactions between civilizations across continents.

Embark on this journey through time and witness how Alexander's conquests shaped the world we live in today.

As Alexander's empire expanded, the interconnectedness of different civilizations began to take shape, laying the foundation for early forms of globalization. The cultural exchanges facilitated by Alexander's conquests played a crucial role in shaping the world as we know it today. *These exchanges shared ideas, goods, and traditions among the Greeks, Egyptians, Persians, and Indians,* creating a melting pot of diversity and innovation. This cross-pollination of cultures enriched the societies involved and paved the way for a more interconnected world.

The interactions between these civilizations led to a blending of customs and beliefs, sparking a cultural renaissance that transcended geographical boundaries. The knowledge exchange in science, philosophy, and art fostered intellectual growth and creativity. *Innovations spread rapidly across regions,* leading to advancements that might not have been possible in isolation. The interconnectedness forged during this era laid the groundwork for future collaborations and mutual understanding among diverse peoples.

Trade flourished due to increased connectivity, with goods flowing along established trade routes crisscrossing Alexander's vast empire. The Silk Road, for example, became a conduit for the exchange of commodities between East and West, further solidifying the ties between distant lands. *Economic prosperity followed in the wake of these trade networks,* bolstering the stability and growth of the regions involved. The interconnectedness fostered by Alexander's conquests created a web of economic interdependence that benefited all parties involved.

Cultural diffusion was not one-sided but rather a reciprocal exchange, with each civilization contributing its unique perspectives and practices to the collective pool of knowledge. This cross-cultural fertilization led to a rich tapestry of ideas and traditions transcending individual identities. *The blending of cultures resulted in hybrid societies that embraced diversity and* celebrated the richness of human experience. This fusion of customs and beliefs laid the groundwork for tolerance and acceptance, fostering a spirit of inclusivity that transcended borders.

The interconnectedness forged during this period set the stage for future interactions between civilizations, paving the way for a more globalized world. The seeds planted by Alexander's conquests blossomed into a shared heritage that transcended national boundaries, uniting diverse peoples under a standard banner of humanity. *The impacts of these early forms of globalization continue to resonate today,* shaping our interconnected world and reminding us of the enduring legacy of cultural exchange.

As we delve into the long-term impacts of the cultural exchanges initiated by Alexander the Great, it becomes evident that these interactions had a profound and lasting influence on his empire and the regions beyond. *One significant outcome* was blending diverse cultures, leading to a rich tapestry of shared knowledge, traditions, and innovations. This fusion enriched the societies involved and laid the foundation for future advancements in various fields.

The amalgamation of Greek, Egyptian, Persian, and Indian cultures fostered a spirit of collaboration and cross-pollination of ideas that transcended borders. This cultural osmosis sparked creativity and ingenuity, giving rise to new artistic expressions, architectural styles, scientific discoveries, and philosophical insights. *The knowledge exchange* between these civilizations resulted in an intellectual renaissance that propelled advancements in literature, medicine, astronomy, and mathematics.

Moreover, these cultural exchanges played a pivotal role in shaping societal norms and values across different regions. ***The shared experiences fostered*** mutual understanding and tolerance among diverse populations, laying the groundwork for peaceful coexistence and diplomatic relations. ***The legacy*** of this cultural integration can still be seen today in the languages spoken, the religions practiced, and the customs observed in many parts of the world.

On a broader scale, Alexander's promotion of cultural exchanges set a precedent for globalization long before the term was coined. ***His efforts*** to connect distant lands through trade routes and diplomatic missions established a framework for future interactions between nations. This interconnectedness not only facilitated economic growth but also paved the way for greater cultural exchange and cooperation on a global scale.

The enduring impact of Alexander's cultural exchanges can be felt in modern-day society through the interconnected nature of our world. ***The lessons learned from*** this era of cultural fusion serve as a reminder of the power of collaboration and dialogue in overcoming differences and building a more harmonious world. By embracing diversity and celebrating shared heritage, we can continue to honor the legacy of those who came before us and forge a path toward a more united future.

The Pathway of Pioneering Exchanges

Alexander the Great's legacy extends far beyond his battlefield victories, embodying a profound cultural exploration and integration journey. This chapter systematically explored how Alexander's conquests catalyzed artistic discovery and exchange, which, in turn, fostered an unprecedented level of interconnectedness among diverse civilizations.

Step 1: Exploring the Role of Alexander's Conquests in Cultural Discovery and Exchange

Starting with the conquests themselves, Alexander's campaigns were not mere military endeavors but instrumental in bridging diverse cultures. Under his empire, the merging of Greek, Egyptian, Persian, and Indian customs and ideas enhanced cultural understanding and set the stage for a shared global heritage. This initial step was crucial, laying the groundwork for the cultural synthesis that characterized his empire.

Step 2: Analyzing the Influence of Cultural Exchanges on Interconnectedness

Next, we observed how they significantly reduced barriers between civilizations by analyzing the depth of these cultural exchanges. These interactions led to an early form of globalization, where exchanging goods, technologies, and ideologies brought distant cultures into closer contact. This phase was critical in illustrating how Alexander's influence knit a tapestry of cultural cohesion that spanned continents.

Step 3: Evaluating the Long-Term Impacts of Cultural Exchanges

Finally, evaluating the long-term impacts of these exchanges revealed their enduring legacy on art, philosophy, science, and governance. The blend of Greek and Eastern elements can still be seen in various cultural expressions that influence our world today.

This evaluation was essential in understanding how the foundations laid by Alexander's era continued to support artistic and intellectual advancements long after his empire faded.

Through this structured exploration—starting with discovery and moving through interconnectedness to lasting impact—we see that Alexander's true greatness may well lie in his role as a facilitator of cultural fusion. His vision of an empire united by power and respect for diverse cultures helped sow the seeds of modern globalization.

This narrative serves as a testament to Alexander's extraordinary leadership and a reminder of the power of cultural exchange. It encourages us to appreciate our diverse histories and to continue building bridges between cultures. The story of Alexander teaches us that real strength lies in our ability to learn from each other and grow together—a lesson as relevant today as it was over two millennia ago.

Chapter 9: Echoes in Modernity: Geopolitics and Cultural Strategies

The Echoes of Alexander in Modern Diplomacy

It was a crisp autumn morning in the heart of Washington, D.C., where trees stood as silent witnesses to the passage of time and power. James, a seasoned diplomat with a keen interest in historical strategies, walked the well-worn paths of Lafayette Square. His mind buzzed with thoughts of an upcoming international cultural summit. He was tasked with forging a cohesive cultural strategy among diverse nations, each jealously guarding its heritage yet yearning for global integration.

James reflected on Alexander the Great's methods of integrating vast and varied cultures under his dominion as he strolled past the statues that gazed solemnly across the square. He thought about how Alexander didn't just conquer; he also understood and often adopted elements of each local culture, weaving them into his empire's fabric to foster loyalty and unity.

The rustling leaves brought him back from ancient Babylonia to modern geopolitics. The challenge was daunting: how could he apply these ancient lessons to today's complex cultural landscape?

The idea that solutions to contemporary problems might be found in ancient history comforted and overwhelmed him.

Later that day, seated in his office surrounded by books and papers, James poured over accounts of Alexander's strategies at Gaugamela and beyond. The sun dipped low, casting long shadows across his desk cluttered with notes and coffee cups. He scribbled down thoughts feverishly—how cultural respect coupled with strategic governance formed pillars upon which vast territories stood united under Alexander.

A young intern knocked timidly on his open door, bringing in a gust of fresh air that scattered some papers off the desk. *"Excuse me, Mr. Hamilton,"* she said cautiously, *"the ambassador from India is on line one for you."*

James thanked her and picked up the receiver, his mind still half in ancient Macedonia. As he discussed preparing for the ambassador's visit during the summit, he realized this was more than mere diplomacy; it was an opportunity to bridge cultures using time-tested wisdom.

Could understanding Alexander's approach provide a blueprint for solving today's global cultural challenges?

Could the Past Hold the Keys to Modern Global Strategies?

When we delve into the annals of history, Alexander the Great looms as a colossal architect of geopolitical and cultural landscapes. Though millennia old, his governance and cultural integration strategies offer not just a window into ancient tactics but also provide a reflective surface for modern strategy. This chapter aims to thread Alexander's ancient practices with the fabric of contemporary global policies and cultural diplomacy.

Alexander's empire, sprawling from Greece to the far reaches of India, is a fascinating case study for understanding how diverse cultures can be managed under a single political umbrella.

Considering how his approaches might align with or inform today's international relations and strategies in cultural integration is intriguing. Here, we examine ***how historical insights can illuminate modern practices***, potentially guiding current leaders and scholars in navigating our complex global landscape.

We'll first explore ***the linkage between Alexander's governance tactics and today's geopolitical maneuvers***. How did Alexander manage to control such a vast territory, and what can that teach us about power dynamics on the modern world stage? Reflecting on this can provide valuable lessons in leadership and strategy applicable in politics, business, and organizational management.

Next, we'll discuss how Alexander's approach to managing diverse cultures under his empire provides insights into ***modern diplomacy and governance***. His policy of founding cities to spread Greek culture and influence, alongside respecting and incorporating local customs and traditions, offers a dual strategy that echoes today's cultural diplomacy initiatives. This balance between globalization and regional autonomy is more relevant than ever in our interconnected world.

Furthermore, evaluating Alexander's strategies' effectiveness in light of today's international relations offers a chance to critically assess his methods' sustainability and ethical dimensions.

Was his success merely the result of military might, or were there aspects of his cultural strategies that contributed to a more durable impact? Understanding this can help modern policymakers gauge which historical strategy might be practical or ethical in contemporary contexts.

This reflective journey through Alexander's strategies isn't just an academic exercise; it has practical implications for today's understanding of power structures, cultural policies, and corporate governance. By examining these ancient methods, we gain insights into creating more harmonious societies through informed leadership and thoughtful integration of diverse cultural perspectives.

This chapter aims to uncover historical tactics and inspire current and future leaders by demonstrating how ancient wisdom can inform modern strategies. The goal is to foster a deeper understanding of how past empires navigated complexities similar to those we face today, providing valuable lessons that transcend time.

In essence, by looking back at Alexander's legacy, we are not just learning about history but exploring potential pathways for our future geopolitical and cultural endeavors. This exploration encourages us to reflect on past successes and failures and apply these lessons innovatively within our modern contexts.

Alexander the Great's tactics in governance and culture continue to resonate in contemporary geopolitical and cultural strategies. His approach to managing diverse cultures and regions under a single empire provides valuable insights for modern leaders and scholars.

By studying Alexander's methods, we can better understand the complexities of governing diverse populations and integrating cultural norms. The lessons from his empire serve as a foundational blueprint for navigating today's complex geopolitical landscape and fostering cultural diplomacy on a global scale.

Alexander's Legacy in Governance: One key aspect of Alexander's governance that stands out is his ability to adapt to the unique characteristics of each region he conquered. Instead of imposing a uniform system, he displayed flexibility by incorporating local customs and traditions into his administration.

This strategy allowed him to maintain stability and gain the loyalty of the diverse populations under his rule. This approach mirrors modern efforts to respect cultural diversity in governance, emphasizing the importance of understanding and valuing different perspectives.

Cultural Integration Strategies: Alexander's empire was a melting pot of various cultures, religions, and languages. He encouraged cultural exchange and interaction among his subjects, promoting tolerance and mutual respect. This inclusive approach fostered a sense of unity among diverse groups, contributing to the longevity of his empire. ***In today's globalized world, promoting cultural understanding and dialogue remains essential for building strong international relations.***

Geopolitical Insights: Alexander's conquests reshaped the geopolitical landscape of his time, establishing connections between East and West that had lasting effects. His ability to navigate complex alliances, manage vast territories, and project power across borders offers valuable lessons for modern geopolitics. *His challenges in balancing military might with diplomatic finesse are still relevant today in navigating international relations.*

Strategic Adaptability: One of Alexander's greatest strengths was his adaptability in changing circumstances. He displayed agility in adjusting his tactics based on the terrain, enemy strengths, and available resources. This flexibility enabled him to overcome formidable challenges and emerge victorious in many battles.

Modern leaders can learn from this skill by being open to innovation and willing to pivot when necessary.

Explore further how Alexander's multifaceted approach can offer profound insights into navigating the complexities of contemporary geopolitics and cultural diplomacy.

By delving into Alexander the Great's governance and cultural integration methods, we uncover timeless principles that continue to shape our understanding of leadership, diplomacy, and cross-cultural interactions. As we examine his legacy through a modern lens, we can draw inspiration from his strategic insight and visionary leadership to address the intricate challenges of our interconnected world today.

Alexander the Great's approach to managing diverse cultures under a single empire offers valuable insights into modern diplomacy and governance. His ability to blend different traditions, languages, and customs into a cohesive system provides a blueprint for handling multicultural challenges in today's world. *By studying Alexander's methods,* contemporary leaders can learn how to navigate the complexities of cultural integration and geopolitical strategies.

One key lesson from Alexander's empire is the importance of adapting governance to suit the needs of diverse populations.

Instead of imposing a uniform system on all territories, he respected local customs. He appointed officials from various backgrounds to govern effectively. *This flexible approach* ensured stability and loyalty among his subjects, fostering a sense of inclusivity within his vast empire.

Moreover, Alexander's emphasis on cultural exchange and mutual understanding laid the foundation for successful diplomatic relations. *His policy of encouraging intercultural communication* promoted harmony among different ethnic groups and facilitated trade and cooperation. In today's globalized world, this principle remains relevant as nations strive to build bridges and foster collaboration across borders.

Another valuable insight from Alexander's reign is the significance of strong leadership in maintaining unity among diverse cultures. He earned their loyalty and admiration by leading by example and respecting all his subjects. *His charisma and vision* inspired people from various backgrounds to work together towards common goals, showcasing the power of effective leadership in uniting diverse communities.

Additionally, Alexander's strategic alliances with local rulers and integration of foreign practices into his administration illustrate the benefits of embracing diversity in governance. *His willingness to learn from different cultures* and incorporate their innovations into his empire enhanced its strength and resilience. This adaptable approach can serve as a model for modern leaders seeking to leverage diversity as a source of strength in their governance structures.

In conclusion, Alexander the Great's legacy offers timeless lessons for navigating the complexities of managing diverse cultures under a single political framework. *His inclusive policies*, emphasis on cultural exchange, and strong leadership provide valuable insights for contemporary leaders grappling with similar challenges in diplomacy and governance. Drawing inspiration from his strategies, today's decision-makers can build more cohesive societies celebrating diversity while working towards common objectives.

Conceptual Model in Systems Theory

Military Conquests: This component represents Alexander's military campaigns and conquests as the foundation of his empire. By swiftly and decisively conquering territories, Alexander expanded his dominion and asserted his authority over diverse regions. The military conquests were the initial step in establishing control but also necessitated subsequent governance and cultural integration strategies.

Cultural Integration: Cultural integration highlights Alexander's approach to assimilating diverse cultures into his empire. Rather than imposing a singular culture, Alexander embraced the customs and traditions of conquered peoples, fostering a sense of unity amidst diversity. This component emphasizes the importance of respecting and incorporating local practices to maintain stability and harmony within the empire.

Administrative Governance: The administrative governance aspect signifies the bureaucratic structure that enabled Alexander to govern his vast empire efficiently. Establishing administrative centers, appointing officials, and implementing policies were crucial for maintaining order and ensuring the empire's effective functioning. This component illustrates the significance of organizational frameworks in sustaining complex political entities.

Interconnectedness: These components are interconnected in a dynamic system where military conquests lay the groundwork for cultural integration, which, in turn, informs administrative governance. The feedback loops between these elements emphasize how each aspect influences and shapes the others, creating a holistic approach to empire-building.

Dynamics: Over time, this model demonstrates how successful cultural integration enhances loyalty among diverse populations, leading to stability and prosperity within the empire. The equilibrium state is achieved when governance structures effectively balance military conquests with cultural assimilation, fostering a cohesive society.

Practical Implications: This conceptual model offers insights into governance strategies prioritizing cultural sensitivity and inclusivity in modern contexts. Contemporary leaders can navigate diverse geopolitical landscapes more effectively by understanding the interconnectedness of military actions, cultural integration, and administrative governance.

This model underscores the importance of adapting governance approaches to accommodate cultural diversity, promoting harmonious coexistence and sustainable development. By recognizing the interplay between military conquests and cultural integration, leaders can foster mutual understanding and cooperation on a global scale for more stable international relations.

Understanding Alexander the Great enriches our grasp of past empires and illuminates the underpinnings of current global strategies. Throughout this exploration, we have linked Alexander's innovative approaches to governance and cultural assimilation with the nuanced practices of contemporary geopolitics and cultural diplomacy. His legacy offers a timeless blueprint that, even today, can guide leaders and scholars through the intricate dance of international relations.

Alexander's strategic integration of diverse cultures under one dominion reveals much about the power of inclusive governance. Though ancient, this method resonates deeply with today's efforts to foster unity in diversity within globalized settings. Reflecting on Alexander's empire, we see a precursor to modern strategies that seek harmony and cooperation among differing national, ethnic, and cultural groups.

Moreover, ***evaluating Alexander's tactics*** through the lens of today's diplomatic and cultural challenges underscores their enduring relevance. While the contexts may differ drastically, the essence of his strategies—such as forging alliances and understanding cultural nuances—remains pertinent. These actions are not just relics of history but lessons on the effectiveness of empathy and strategic thinking in governance.

As we move forward, let us carry the wisdom from Alexander's era. His story encourages us to be bold in our aspirations and thoughtful in our actions. It teaches us that leadership is not merely about conquest but about leaving a legacy of interconnectedness and respect across different cultures.

In drawing lessons from the past, we pay homage to significant historical figures like Alexander and empower ourselves to craft a future that echoes the best of human values and strategies. As we continue our journey through history, let this chapter serve as a reminder of how deeply our present is entwined with the threads of the past, urging us to build on this knowledge with courage and foresight.

Chapter 10: Visionary Leadership: Changing the World One Empire at a Time

Visionary Shadows in the Halls of Power

In the dim light of early morning, Thomas walked through the deserted corridors of the parliament building. The echoes of his footsteps mingled with the weighty silence that filled the vast hallways—a silence that seemed to hold its breath, anticipating change. Today, Thomas was to deliver a speech that could pivot his career towards a trajectory he had long envisioned, inspired by the histories of great leaders like Alexander.

His mind wandered to Alexander's relentless pursuit of his vision—an empire stretched across continents, cultures blending under one rule. Thomas had studied this for academic adornment and as a blueprint for modern governance. He imagined a society where different voices merged into a harmonious symphony rather than clashing cymbals. His heart raced with the possibility as he adjusted his tie, catching his reflection in one of the grand hallway mirrors.

He paused before an old painting depicting Alexander at Gaugamela, determination etched into every brush stroke. Thomas felt a kinship across time—a shared heartbeat between those destined to lead, to change courses of rivers and nations alike. *"With vision and determination,"* he whispered, recalling lines from an old text about how such traits could change the world.

A young aide approached him with papers, breaking his reverie. *"Sir, your notes for today."* The crisp rustle of paper brought him back from ancient battlefields to polished wood and marble halls.

As he reviewed his speech, doubts crept in like shadows at dusk—was his vision too grand? Would his words find fertile ground or fall on barren soil? His proposal was bold: an international coalition for environmental and economic cooperation unlike any before it. It was designed to address current issues and prevent future crises—a preventive war against disaster.

Thomas continued down the corridor toward the chamber where history would either embrace or turn away from him. His steps slowed as he pondered whether today's decisions would be remembered as fondly as those made millennia ago by great leaders like Alexander.

Will our modern society understand and accept visionary leadership as it did in ancient times?

Vision Meets Reality: How Alexander the Great's Dream Changed the World

Alexander the Great's life is often heralded for its military genius and vast conquests, but beneath the armor and beyond the battlefield lay a visionary leader whose ambitions reshaped the known world. This chapter delves into how Alexander's vision of a united empire changed geographical boundaries and influenced leadership models for centuries. His strategy, persistence, and visionary outlook offer timeless lessons in leadership, particularly in the realms of vision and determination.

At the heart of Alexander's success was his exceptional ability to *envision a reality far beyond the immediate grasp* of his contemporaries. He did not see Asia as a land to conquer but as a potential domain under a unified empire, blending diverse cultures and economies into a powerful entity. This chapter will explore how this vision drove him from one victory to another, often in the face of overwhelming odds.

Equally crucial was his relentless pursuit of this vision. Alexander's campaigns, which stretched from Greece through Asia Minor, Egypt, and India, showcase his tactical brilliance and unwavering commitment to his goals. This chapter will draw parallels between Alexander's pursuit and contemporary leadership practices, highlighting how *modern leaders can harness similar focus and resilience* in their ventures.

Furthermore, this exploration underscores the importance of having a vision and the tenacity to follow through. Alexander's ability to dream big and act decisively turned potential into reality—a lesson vital for today's leaders in any field. The discussion here aims to illuminate how transformative changes can be achieved when leaders commit wholeheartedly to their visions.

Reflecting on these themes ties together the overarching narratives of this book: understanding Alexander not just as a military figure but as a transformative leader who left an indelible mark on history through his vision and action. By examining these facets of his leadership, readers gain insights into historical strategies and contemporary applications relevant to various spheres of influence today.

In essence, by studying Alexander's leadership approach, we learn about more than just ancient tactics; we uncover principles of visionary leadership that can inspire and guide current and future leaders across the globe. This chapter sets out to equip readers with knowledge that empowers them to apply these time-tested strategies in their professional lives, encouraging them to pursue their visions with similar vigor and determination.

As we move forward, remember that understanding such a colossal figure requires viewing him through multiple lenses—military genius, cultural amalgamator, and visionary leader. Each perspective offers unique insights that contribute to a fuller comprehension of his impact—a synthesis of ideas shaping our interpretation of leadership. Through this holistic exploration, readers are invited to admire Alexander's accomplishments and extract practical lessons that resonate with their personal and professional aspirations.

Alexander's leadership was marked by a visionary outlook that propelled him to create one of the most extensive empires in history.

His ability to see beyond the immediate horizon and envision a world united under his rule set him apart as a leader of unparalleled ambition. *Alexander's vision was not limited to mere conquest; it extended to establishing a new world order where diverse cultures could coexist and flourish under a standard banner.* This far-reaching vision guided his decisions, from strategic military campaigns to diplomatic negotiations, shaping history's course in ways few could have imagined.

The empire Alexander forged was a collection of conquered lands and a testament to his belief in unity through diversity. By incorporating various customs, traditions, and beliefs into his empire, he demonstrated remarkable tolerance and inclusivity for his time. *His vision encompassed territorial expansion, cultural exchange, and mutual understanding among different peoples.* This holistic approach to empire-building set Alexander apart as a leader seeking power, dominion, harmony, and cooperation among nations.

One of the critical aspects of Alexander's visionary leadership was his ability to inspire others to share in his grand vision. He rallied troops from diverse backgrounds around a common purpose through his charisma, charisma, and personal magnetism, instilling a sense of belonging to something greater than themselves. *His ability to communicate his vision effectively and motivate others to act on it was instrumental in the success of his campaigns.* By fostering a sense of shared destiny among his followers, Alexander created a formidable force capable of achieving the seemingly impossible.

Alexander's vision went beyond mere conquest; it aimed at transforming the world into a more interconnected and harmonious place. His dream of uniting East and West, bridging cultural divides, and fostering cooperation among nations reflects a profound understanding of the power of visionary leadership. *His legacy serves as a reminder that with a clear vision and unwavering determination, leaders can transcend boundaries and bring about positive change on a global scale.*

Alexander's unwavering commitment to his vision of a vast empire holds valuable lessons for contemporary leaders. His relentless pursuit of conquering new territories and uniting diverse cultures under his rule showcases the power of determination and focus in achieving ambitious goals. In today's fast-paced world, where distractions abound, and obstacles seem insurmountable, Alexander's example serves as a beacon of inspiration. *Despite* facing numerous challenges and setbacks, his dedication to his vision highlights the importance of perseverance in leadership.

In the modern context, leaders often encounter complexities that can deter them from their objectives. However, by embodying Alexander's unwavering spirit, they can navigate turbulent times with resilience and courage. *Staying true to one's vision* despite adversity distinguishes exceptional leaders. *By drawing parallels between Alexander's unwavering determination and* contemporary leadership practices, individuals can glean insights on how to stay focused amidst chaos and uncertainty.

Alexander's legacy underscores the significance of adaptability in leadership. While he had a grand vision of empire-building, he also displayed flexibility in his strategies when faced with new challenges. This adaptability allowed him to navigate diverse terrains and adjust his tactics according to the changing circumstances. *In today's dynamic business environment*, where agility is critical to success, leaders can learn from Alexander's ability to pivot when necessary while keeping sight of their overarching goals.

Moreover, Alexander's leadership exemplifies the importance of bold decision-making. His willingness to take risks and venture into unknown territories demonstrates the value of daring choices in driving progress. *By embracing calculated risks*, leaders can propel their organizations forward and seize opportunities for growth and innovation. *Alexander's fearlessness in the face of uncertainty* serves as a reminder that outstanding achievements often require stepping out of one's comfort zone.

The essence of visionary leadership lies in the ability to inspire others towards a common goal. Alexander's charisma and magnetic personality drew people to his cause, creating a sense of unity among diverse followers. His capacity to rally support and instill a shared sense of purpose enabled him to achieve feats that seemed impossible then. *Today's leaders can emulate this aspect* by cultivating strong relationships, fostering collaboration, and articulating a compelling vision that resonates with their teams.

Ultimately, Alexander's story is a testament to the transformative power of visionary leadership. His unwavering commitment to his grand vision, adaptability, bold decision-making, and ability to inspire others showcases a blueprint for driving change on a global scale. By embracing these principles, contemporary leaders can channel their inner conquerors and embark on their greatness quest.

The legacy of Alexander the Great serves as a timeless guide, reminding us that with vision, determination, and courage, we, too, can leave an indelible mark on the world.

Drawing Lessons from Alexander's Legacy

Reflecting on Alexander the Great's life, we can glean valuable insights into the importance of vision and determination in driving transformative change. Alexander's unwavering commitment to his vision of a vast empire is a poignant reminder of the power of having a clear goal and the resilience to pursue it relentlessly. *His legacy underscores the significance of setting ambitious yet achievable goals and staying dedicated to their realization despite obstacles and challenges.*

Visionary leaders like Alexander inspire us to dream big and work tirelessly towards those dreams, even when the path ahead seems daunting. They remind us that true transformation often requires stepping out of our comfort zones, embracing uncertainty, and persisting in adversity. *By learning from Alexander's example, we can cultivate a mindset focused on long-term goals rather than immediate gratification,* understanding that meaningful change often takes time, effort, and unwavering resolve.

The lessons from Alexander's legacy extend beyond conquering lands; they delve into personal growth and leadership development. Emulating his visionary approach involves envisioning grand possibilities and honing the skills necessary to realize those visions. *Leaders who aspire to effect transformative change must cultivate strategic thinking, adaptability, and resilience,* embodying a steadfast commitment to their goals while remaining open to new opportunities and feedback.

Alexander's legacy challenges us to push beyond our perceived limitations and embrace discomfort as a catalyst for growth. His audacity in pursuing his vision is a testament to the transformative power of bold action and unwavering determination. *By internalizing these lessons, we can embark on our journeys of self-discovery and leadership development,* guided by a deep sense of purpose and an unyielding drive to positively impact the world around us.

In essence, Alexander's story reminds us that transformative change begins with a clear vision but is sustained through perseverance and resilience. His legacy invites us to reimagine our potential for greatness, urging us to set audacious goals and pursue them with unwavering determination. *By embracing these lessons from history, we can navigate the complexities of modern leadership with clarity, purpose, and steadfast resolve* inspired by the enduring legacy of one of history's most visionary leaders.

Alexander the Great's vision was a fleeting dream and a transformative force that reshaped the ancient world. His leadership, driven by a clear and compelling vision, demonstrates the profound impact that a single individual's determination and foresight can have on history. Throughout this book, we have explored the intricate details of Alexander's journey, from his tactical prowess on the battlefield to his strategic insight into governance and his role in the cultural amalgamation of the empires he conquered. Each chapter has built upon the next to paint a comprehensive picture of a leader whose legacy is as vast as the territories he once ruled.

Visionary leadership is at the heart of Alexander's success. His ability to see beyond immediate military conquests to the broader implications of his actions offers a timeless lesson in strategic planning and execution. By examining his life, we gain insights into the power of having a clear, ambitious goal. Alexander's story encourages current and future leaders in any field to envision what is possible and to pursue it with unwavering resolve.

The parallels between Alexander's leadership approach and *contemporary practices* are striking. Today's leaders can draw inspiration from their efforts to integrate different cultures and instill a sense of purpose among diverse peoples, His approach underscores the importance of adaptability and visionary thinking in today's globalized world.

Moreover, Alexander's legacy teaches us the importance of *determination and vision*. His relentless pursuit of his goals, often amid enormous challenges, exemplifies the tenacity required to effect substantial change. This blend of vision and perseverance is crucial for anyone who aims to leave a lasting impact on their community or industry.

Reflecting on Alexander's journey helps us understand the transformative power of visionary leadership. It compels us to ask ourselves how deep our convictions are and challenges us to think about how far we are willing to go to realize our visions. His life prompts us to consider our legacies—what we will leave behind and how we can shape the future.

As we close this exploration of Alexander the Great, remember that the lessons drawn from his life are not confined to the annals of history. They are vibrant, living guides that can inspire us to pursue our visions with boldness and determination. Whether you lead a team, a company, or simply your endeavors, integrating the lessons from Alexander's life can propel you toward achieving transformative success.

Let this book be both a map and a compass as you navigate your challenges and opportunities. Embrace the courage to see beyond the horizon, just as Alexander did, and you might find yourself changing the world in ways you never imagined.

Epilogue

Unveiling the Legacy: A Conclusive Reflection

As we draw the curtains on our journey through Alexander the Great's life and times, we must stitch together the vibrant tapestry of narratives, insights, and revelations we've encountered.

Throughout this book, we've traversed vast landscapes both geographically and intellectually, uncovering the layers that compose not only a man but an era that continues to echo through time.

Alexander's strategies and decisions offer more than historical anecdotes; they serve as lessons in leadership, resilience, and vision applicable in various spheres of our modern lives. Whether you're a leader in your community, a strategist in business, or a creative mind seeking inspiration, there's wisdom to glean from Alexander's life. His ability to see beyond the immediate horizons and envision a world united under common ideals can inspire us to think globally in our pursuits and interactions.

Reflecting on the main ideas explored—his unmatched military prowess, profound impact on cultural exchange, and visionary approach—we see a figure who was more than a conqueror. He was a pivotal force in shaping what we now consider the Hellenistic world. His policies on cultural integration, for example, could enlighten today's global leaders on fostering more inclusive societies.

However, like any exploration of history deeply shrouded in both legend and documented fact, this book has limitations. The scarcity of contemporary sources and the romanticism of later writers often blur the lines between the man and the myth. Further research and archaeological advancements may continue to refine our understanding of Alexander's empire and strategies.

I encourage you to read about history and interact with it. Visit museums, engage with online courses about Hellenistic history, or even participate in discussions at local community centers. Use what you've learned here as a springboard for your explorations or as a tool to navigate current global challenges.

Remember that history is not just about the past; it's a continuous dialogue between then and now, influencing how we perceive and shape our future. Let Alexander's legacy inspire you to pursue greatness in your endeavors with boldness and an enduring spirit.

"For I would rather excel others in the knowledge of what is excellent than in the extent of my powers and dominion" - **Alexander the Great**

This quote encapsulates the true essence of his ambitions—not merely to conquer but to excel in understanding and wisdom. May his journey enrich your paths as you pursue your great exploits.

Don't miss out!

Visit the website below and you can sign up to receive emails whenever Myrddin Sage publishes a new book. There's no charge and no obligation.

https://books2read.com/r/B-A-JBAOB-BHMXE

BOOKS 2 READ

Connecting independent readers to independent writers.

About the Author

At 67, Myrddin Sage steps into the spotlight as a newly published author, bringing a tapestry of rich life experiences and a vibrant imagination. His journey from a Navy Veteran to a Retired Dispatcher of Messengers has endowed him with profound insights into human cultures and the natural world. As Myrddin introduces his debut novel, he shares a narrative infused with wisdom, whimsy, and a deep respect for the interconnectedness of life. Drawing on his academic background and extensive travels, Myrddin's work explores themes of adventure, discovery, and the transformative power of knowledge. With his first publication, he proves that new chapters can be embarked upon at any stage of life, inspiring readers with the message that it is always the right time to follow one's passions.